Norse Mythology, Legends and Legacy

Embark on an Exciting Journey

into Viking Lore,

Uncover the Myths of Odin, Thor and Loki

Thru Engaging Storytelling

and Modern Insights

D1522590

Shari Claire

First edition
ISBN 979-8339012474

Table of Contents

Introduction

The towering figures of Norse mythology stand in the shadowy realms of ancient lore, where the line between the human and the divine blurs. These tales are not just stories but a testament to life's struggles, triumphs, and enduring mysteries. The gods, giants, and heroes of old—Odin, Thor, Loki, and many others—invite you into a world where the epic sagas of love, betrayal, and adventure reveal the complexities of the human heart intertwined with the supernatural.

This book is crafted with a dual purpose: to serve as a bridge connecting the scholarly depth of Norse mythology with the engaging clarity of modern storytelling. It aims to guide you through the intricate narratives and profound themes that have shaped Viking culture, resonating through the ages to touch our lives today.

Our journey will include meticulously detailed accounts of the major Norse gods, enhanced by an in-depth analysis of themes such as creation, destiny, and the cataclysmic Ragnarok.

With their rich tapestry of magic, heroism, and moral inquiry, Norse myths continue to captivate and influence contemporary society, from arts and literature to philosophical discourse. Understanding these ancient stories enriches our comprehension of the past and the cultural and ethical underpinnings of modern civilization.

My own journey into the heart of these myths has been one of passion and discovery. From a young enthusiast of legendary tales who reveled in the stories of gods and monsters, I have grown into a dedicated scholar seeking to share these wonders in an informative and captivating form. This book is the culmination of that quest, aimed at demystifying the complex world of Norse gods and heroes for an audience that ranges from the casual reader to the academic scholar.

This book is designed to appeal to mythology enthusiasts, history buffs, fantasy fans, and scholars alike. Whether you are deeply knowledgeable about Norse mythology or newly curious about the tales of Viking gods and heroes, you will find valuable insights and entertaining stories here.

Structured to provide a comprehensive exploration, the book delves into the pantheon of Norse gods and the far-reaching influence of their stories. Each chapter is crafted to enhance your understanding and appreciation of this rich mythology, ensuring a balanced blend of educational depth and compelling narrative.

Join me on this fascinating journey through the myths that have shaped centuries of storytelling, philosophy, and culture. Let us explore together the profound lessons these ancient stories hold for the modern world. May you find, as I have, a deep and enduring appreciation for the intricate tapestry of Norse mythology.

Chapter 1:

ASGARD · VADAHEIM · ADGARD · JOTCHEIM · IITAREIM · YUDOARM · VALHI · MUSTELHEIR · YUTHEII · MUSTCHEIM · MUSIALHEIM · YOLDAHEIM · HUSLHEIM

The Pantheon of Norse Gods

Imagine a world suspended in the branches of a colossal and ever-growing tree known as Yggdrasil, the World Tree. This immense ash tree is not merely a part of the landscape but the very backbone of Norse cosmology, a living structure that connects the nine distinct worlds and embodies the cyclical nature of life, death, and rebirth. Each leaf rustles with the whispers of ancient secrets, and every root delves deep into the mysteries of existence. In this intricate and mythical landscape, the realm of Asgard stands tall and majestic among the highest branches, serving as the divine abode of the Aesir gods who govern the cosmos with wisdom, might, and occasionally, intrigue.

At the heart of Asgard lies Valhalla, the grand hall where warriors chosen by the Valkyries reside after heroic deaths in battle. Its walls are adorned with shields, and its ceiling glistens with gilded spear shafts. Here, Odin, the All-Father and the wisest of the gods sits upon his high throne, Hlidskjalf, from which he can observe all that transpires in the nine realms. Clad in a cloak of midnight blue and accompanied by his ravens Huginn (Thought) and Muninn (Memory), Odin's single eye glows with the wisdom of ages—a sacrifice he made in exchange for profound knowledge at the Well of Mimir.

With its golden halls and shimmering towers reaching toward the heavens, Asgard is a realm of unparalleled beauty and power. Its streets are lined with precious stones, and its gardens bloom with flowers that never fade. Here, the gods convene in the great council chamber to deliberate on matters of fate, justice, and the balance of the cosmos. They celebrate their victories and alliances with lavish feasts, where the mead flows endlessly, and the skalds sing songs of past glories and future prophecies.

Connecting Asgard to Midgard, the world of humans, is the Bifrost, a radiant rainbow bridge guarded vigilantly by Heimdall, the ever-watchful sentinel whose keen senses can detect the softest whisper or the faintest footfall from realms away. The Bifrost is not just a passageway but a symbol of the link between the divine and the mortal, the seen and the unseen. It is the path over which gods tread to influence human affairs, and occasionally, mortals traverse in quests that blur the lines between man and myth.

Within Asgard, deities such as Thor, the mighty protector wielding his hammer Mjölnir, and Freyja, the goddess of love, beauty, fertility, and

4

war, navigate complex relationships and destinies. Thor, revered for his strength and valor, often journeys to Midgard to defend both gods and humans from the chaotic forces of the giants and other malevolent beings. His thunderous chariot, drawn by two goats, rumbles across the skies, symbolizing the storms that both nourish and challenge life below.

Freyja, with her chariot drawn by cats and a cloak of falcon feathers, embodies the dualities of love and war, beauty and sorcery. She is sought after by gods and giants alike, her allure captivating all who behold her. Freyja's tears of red gold enrich the worlds, and her necklace Brísingamen is a treasure of unparalleled craftsmanship, often the object of desire and contention.

Other notable gods include Týr, the one-handed god of law and heroic glory, who sacrificed his hand to bind the monstrous wolf Fenrir; Balder, the radiant god of light and purity whose tragic death foretells the coming of Ragnarök; and Loki, the cunning trickster whose mischief brings both aid and ruin to gods and men. Loki's complex lineage and shape-shifting abilities make him a figure of both fascination and fear, embodying the unpredictable forces of chaos and change.

At the base of Yggdrasil lies the Well of Urd, shrouded in mist and profound mystery. It is tended by the Norns—three powerful beings named Urd (Past), Verdandi (Present), and Skuld (Future)—who weave the threads of fate for gods and mortals alike on their great loom. The well is a convergence point where past actions influence present circumstances, and future possibilities are spun into the tapestry of existence. The Norns' ceaseless weaving determines the destiny of all beings, and not even the gods can escape their decrees.

Nearby, the dragon Nidhogg gnaws at the roots of Yggdrasil. At the same time, the eagle Veðrfölnir perches atop its highest branches, representing the eternal struggle between destructive forces and the resilience of life. The squirrel Ratatoskr scurries up and down the trunk, carrying messages—and insults—between Nidhogg and the eagle, symbolizing the flow of gossip and discord that can pervade any society.

The Well of Urd and the eternal growth of Yggdrasil underscore the Norse belief in destiny and the interconnectedness of all things. The tree's three main roots extend into Asgard, Jotunheim (the realm of the giants), and Niflheim (the world of ice and mist), connecting realms of order, chaos, and the primordial elements. Daily, the gods convene at Yggdrasil to hold their councils, acknowledging that despite their immense powers, they are bound by the same cosmic laws and fates that govern all existence.

This grand, living cosmos, with its interwoven realms and eternal cycles, provides a backdrop for the epic tales of heroism, sacrifice, and cosmic balance that define Norse mythology. The stories of gods and giants, heroes and monsters, are not isolated legends but parts of a greater narrative that reflects the values, fears, and aspirations of the Norse people. Themes of honor, courage, and the acceptance of fate permeate these myths, offering insights into the human condition and the mysteries of the universe.

As we delve deeper into the pantheon of Norse gods, we encounter a rich tapestry of deities, each embodying different aspects of life and nature. Njord, the god of the sea and wind, brings prosperity to seafarers and fishermen. His children, Frey and Freyja, are central figures associated with fertility and the bounty of the earth. Skadi, the goddess of winter and hunting, represents the harsh yet beautiful aspects of the natural world. Idun, the guardian of the golden apples, ensures the gods' immortality; her role is critical in maintaining the divine order.

The relationships between these gods are complex and often tumultuous, filled with alliances, rivalries, and profound moments of cooperation and conflict. Their stories are chronicled in the Poetic Edda and Prose Edda, ancient texts that serve as primary sources for Norse mythology.

Through these sagas, we witness the gods' adventures, their interactions with humans, and their preparations for Ragnarök—the prophesied apocalypse that will lead to the renewal of the world.

In the shadow of impending doom, the gods exhibit remarkably human traits: fear, jealousy, love, and honor. They strive to delay the inevitable, knowing their efforts may ultimately be in vain. Yet, in this struggle, they find purpose and meaning, embodying the Norse ethos of facing one's destiny with courage and dignity.

The Pantheon of Norse Gods is not just a collection of deities but a reflection of a worldview that embraces the complexities of existence. It acknowledges the interplay between order and chaos, the transient nature of life, and the enduring quest for knowledge and understanding. As we embark on this exploration of Norse mythology, we are invited to contemplate these themes and consider their relevance in our own lives.

Through the sagas of Odin's quest for wisdom, Thor's battles against giants, and Freyja's search for her lost husband Óðr, we gain insights into the values that shaped Viking society. The importance of honor, the significance of oaths and promises, and the recognition of the interconnectedness of all things are lessons woven into the fabric of these myths.

As we stand at the foot of Yggdrasil and gaze upon the splendor of Asgard, we begin a journey into a world where the divine and mortal realms intertwine, where heroes rise and fall, and where the threads of fate are spun by hands both mysterious and mighty. The Pantheon of Norse Gods beckons us to explore the depths of their stories, uncover the wisdom hidden within, and marvel at the enduring legacy of a mythology that continues to captivate and inspire.

7

Odin's Quest for Wisdom

Odin, the All-Father, was the king of the Aesir gods and a seeker of profound wisdom and knowledge. Among his many quests, one stands out for its sheer determination and the ultimate sacrifice it required: his journey to obtain the secrets of the runes.

Odin's journey begins with the Yggdrasil, the immense ash tree that connects all nine worlds. At the roots of this sacred tree lies the Well of Mimir, guarded by the wise and mysterious Mimir himself. It was said that the waters of this well contained vast wisdom and knowledge, but such wisdom came at a great price.

Determined to gain this knowledge, Odin approached Mimir and requested a drink from the well. Knowing the value of what he guarded,

Mimir demanded a significant sacrifice in return. Without hesitation, Odin gouged out one of his eyes and dropped it into the well, signifying his willingness to give up part of himself for the greater good.

The pursuit of wisdom did not end at Mimir's well. Odin sought the knowledge of the runes—ancient symbols that held the secrets of the universe and the power to influence fate. To uncover these mysteries, Odin subjected himself to one of the most arduous trials.

He hung himself from a branch of Yggdrasil, pierced by his own spear, Gungnir. For nine days and nine nights, he hung there, teetering on the brink of death, without food or water. This self-sacrifice was not only a physical ordeal but a spiritual journey into the depths of existence.

On the ninth night, as he stared into the abyss, the secrets of the runes were revealed to Odin. The symbols appeared before him, each one imbued with magical properties and profound meanings. These runes granted him immense power, from healing wounds to influencing events and communicating with spirits.

With this newfound wisdom, Odin enhanced his abilities and shared this knowledge with humanity, teaching them how to use the runes for protection, healing, and divination.

Odin's quest for wisdom underscores the recurring themes of sacrifice and the relentless pursuit of knowledge in Norse mythology. His willingness to endure pain and loss for the greater good exemplifies the Vikings' values: bravery, resilience, and the ceaseless quest for understanding.

The story of Odin's sacrifice teaches us that true wisdom often requires great personal cost and the pursuit of knowledge is a journey filled with trials and tribulations. Yet, it also offers the promise of immense rewards, not just for oneself but for all who follow.

By embracing these lessons, we are reminded of the importance of striving for knowledge and understanding, no matter the cost. Odin's tale continues to inspire, urging us to seek deeper truths and to face our own challenges with courage and determination.

The Legacy

Reflect on the themes of power, wisdom, and sacrifice, as we learned in Odin's relentless quest for knowledge, even at the cost of his own eye. This narrative is not just tales of divine exploits but profound explorations of the values and beliefs that shaped Norse culture. Odin's sacrifice at Mimir's well, where he gives up one of his eyes to gain the wisdom of the ages, symbolizes pursuing knowledge at great personal cost. This act of self-sacrifice underscores the importance the Norse placed on wisdom and the lengths to which one might go to attain it.

Odin's narratives are filled with paradoxes. He is a war god who seeks peace, a poet who thrives in chaos, and a sage who delves into the unknown. His dual nature is reflected in his many names and roles, including the "Father of the Slain" for his association with warriors who die bravely in battle and are taken to Valhalla, his majestic hall. Valhalla is not just a place of honor but a preparation ground for the final battle of Ragnarok, where Odin's chosen warriors, the Einherjar, will fight by his side. Odin's multifaceted character, encompassing both creation and destruction, wisdom and warfare, makes him one of the most complex and revered figures in Norse mythology.

Thor: The Thunderer

Next, we meet Thor, the god of thunder, whose strength is legendary. Thor's hammer, Mjölnir, is a weapon of immense power and a symbol of protection for gods and humans alike. This mighty hammer, capable of leveling mountains, always returns to Thor's hand after being thrown, underscoring his unparalleled might and reliability. His chariot, drawn by two goats, Tanngrisnir and Tanngnjóstr, roars across the skies, bringing thunder and lightning with every journey. This celestial vehicle embodies Thor's connection to the elemental forces of nature and signifies his role as a guardian.

Thor is the embodiment of brute strength and unyielding courage. Unlike Odin's complex and multifaceted nature, Thor's straightforward character makes him a beloved figure among gods and men. He is a protector, always ready to defend Asgard from the giants of Jotunheim and other threats. Thor's fearless nature and unwavering sense of duty endear him to those who seek a champion against chaos and evil. His straightforward approach to problems, relying on his immense physical strength and indomitable spirit, highlights the virtues of honesty, loyalty, and valor.

One of the most famous tales of Thor is his journey to the land of the giants to retrieve his stolen hammer.

The Theft of Mjölnir

The story begins when Thor, the god of thunder and protector of Asgard, awakens to find that his hammer, Mjölnir, is missing. Mjölnir was not just a weapon but a powerful symbol of Thor's strength and a crucial tool for protecting the gods from the forces of chaos, particularly the giants. Thor's first instinct was to seek out Loki, the trickster god, for assistance in recovering the hammer.

Loki, known for his cunning and resourcefulness, quickly agreed to help Thor. The two gods went to Freyja, the goddess of love and beauty, to borrow her magical feathered cloak, which allowed the wearer to transform into a falcon and fly great distances. With Freyja's permission, Loki donned the cloak and set off in search of Mjölnir.

Loki flew across the nine realms, eventually reaching Jotunheim, the land of the giants. There, he encountered Thrym, a powerful giant who revealed that he had stolen Mjölnir and hidden it deep beneath the earth. Thrym declared that he would only return the hammer on one condition: the gods must deliver Freyja to him as his bride.

Loki returned to Asgard with this news, but the gods were outraged at Thrym's demand. Freyja, in particular, was furious at the suggestion that she be given away to a giant. However, without Mjölnir, the gods were vulnerable and needed a plan to recover the hammer.

After much deliberation, Loki devised a plan. He suggested Thor disguise himself as Freyja and travel to Jotunheim to trick Thrym into returning to Mjölnir. Though initially reluctant, Thor agreed to the plan, understanding the importance of recovering his hammer. The gods dressed Thor in Freyja's finest bridal clothes and adorned him with a veil to conceal his face. Loki, ever the schemer, accompanied him, disguised as a handmaiden.

The two gods arrived in Jotunheim, where Thrym enthusiastically greeted them. Believing his demands had been met, he prepared a grand feast to celebrate the wedding. Despite his disguise, Thor could not suppress his godly appetite and devoured an entire ox, eight salmon, and all the delicacies set before him. He even drank three casks of mead, much to the astonishment of the giants.

Thrym, suspicious of his bride's ravenous appetite, questioned Loki, who quickly explained that "Freyja" had not eaten for eight days due to her excitement about the wedding. Thrym accepted this explanation and, eager to formalize the marriage, ordered Mjölnir to be brought out as part of the ceremony.

As Mjölnir was placed on Thor's lap to bless the union, Thor seized the opportunity. He threw off his disguise, revealing his true identity. With a mighty roar, Thor grasped Mjölnir, regaining his full strength and power. In a flash, he struck down Thrym and the other giants at the feast, ensuring they would never threaten the gods again.

Thor and Loki then returned to Asgard, victorious. The gods celebrated the return of Mjölnir, and Thor resumed his role as the protector of Asgard, ever vigilant against the threats from the giants.

The Legacy

This tale, often referred to as "Þrymskviða" or "The Lay of Thrym," emphasizes the value of wit and courage in the face of adversity. It also highlights the significance of Mjölnir, not only as a weapon but as a symbol of divine power and protection. The story remains a timeless reminder of the cunning and strength of the gods, particularly Thor, in safeguarding the cosmos from chaos.

Thor's stories highlight the themes of strength, bravery, and the eternal struggle against chaos. His unwavering dedication to protecting his realm makes him a symbol of resilience and fortitude. Through his relentless battles and acts of protection, Thor embodies the enduring spirit of the warrior, always standing as a bulwark against the encroaching forces of disorder and destruction. His legacy, marked by thunderous victories and heroic feats, inspires those who value strength, courage, and the defense of what is just and good.

Freyja: The Goddess of Love and War

Freyja, the goddess of love, beauty, and war, is one of the most revered figures in Norse mythology. Her dual nature reflects the complex interplay of love and conflict, making her a multifaceted deity who embodies the full spectrum of human experience. Freyja's chariot, pulled by two large cats, symbolizes her connection to both the earthly and the mystical realms. Additionally, her cloak of falcon feathers, which allows her to transform into a bird, signifies her ability to traverse between the physical and spiritual worlds, enhancing her role as a bridge between different aspects of existence.

Freyja is also known for her exquisite necklace, Brísingamen, symbolizing her beauty, power, and status among the gods. Her stories often revolve around themes of desire, wealth, and the quest for power, illustrating the lengths she and others will go to obtain what they desire. Despite her association with love and beauty, Freyja is also a formidable warrior. She claims half of the slain warriors who do not go to Odin's Valhalla, taking them to her own hall, Fólkvangr. This dual role underscores her connection to both creation and destruction, love and war.

The tale of Freyja's search for her lost husband, Óðr, is one of the most touching and evocative stories in Norse mythology. It speaks to the goddess's boundless love, sorrow, and enduring strength in the face of profound loss. This story, rich with emotion and symbolism, portrays Freyja's resilience and the deep connection between love and grief.

The Disappearance of Óðr

Freyja, one of the most revered goddesses in Norse mythology, was deeply devoted to her husband, Óðr. Their union was a harmonious blend of love, passion, and mutual respect, embodying the ideals of companionship and affection. Together, they shared a profound bond filled with joy, laughter, and shared experiences that enriched the realms they touched. Their love was so radiant that it became a beacon, admired by gods and mortals alike.

However, one fateful day, Óðr mysteriously disappeared without a trace. His sudden absence was as if the sun had vanished from the sky, engulfing Freyja in a profound darkness. Bereft and heartbroken, she felt an immense void in her heart that nothing could fill. The halls of Fólkvangr, her heavenly abode, echoed with the silence of his absence, and the once vibrant gardens seemed dull and lifeless without his presence.

Determined to reunite with her beloved, Freyja embarked on an arduous and perilous journey across the nine realms. Clad in her magical cloak of falcon feathers, which allowed her to transform into a falcon, she soared through the skies, traversing vast distances in search of any sign of Óðr. Her quest took her through the dense forests of Midgard, over the

16

towering mountains of Jötunheim, and across the fiery lands of Muspelheim. She braved the chilling winds of Niflheim and ventured into the mysterious depths of Svartalfheim, home of the dwarves, hoping to uncover clues about his whereabouts.

As Freyja wandered in search of Óðr, her sorrow was so intense that her tears turned into gold as they fell from her eyes. These golden tears scattered across the lands, embedding themselves into the earth and rivers, marking the places she had traveled with a lasting testament to her grief and longing. In some tales, these tears also transformed into precious gemstones, such as amber, when they fell into the sea. The people of the realms, upon finding these treasures, were reminded of the goddess's enduring love and the depth of her sorrow.

Her journey was not without challenges. Freyja often encountered obstacles and adversaries who sought to hinder her quest. She faced cunning giants who tried to deceive her, tricky dwarves who demanded high prices for their aid, and even other gods who were indifferent to her plight. Yet, her unwavering determination and the strength of her love empowered her to overcome every hindrance.

In her despair, Freyja sometimes assumed different forms, utilizing her shapeshifting abilities to blend into various environments and gather information. She transformed into birds, beasts, and even other beings, hoping to find clues to Óðr's whereabouts. She consulted with wise beings like the Norns, the weavers of fate, and sought the counsel of seers and oracles, offering them gifts and sacrifices in exchange for any insight. However, even with their vast knowledge and prophetic abilities, the mystery of Óðr's disappearance remained unsolved.

Despite the lack of concrete answers, Freyja never gave up hope. Her love for Óðr was too strong, and her determination to find him kept her going, even as the years passed. During her travels, she occasionally caught fleeting glimpses of Óðr—a shadow moving in the distance, a familiar silhouette disappearing around a corner, or a soft whisper carried by the wind. These moments rekindled her hope, though they were always just out of reach, leaving her longing for a reunion that seemed tantalizingly close yet impossibly far.

Some tales suggest that Óðr's disappearance was a result of his wandering nature. Known to be a restless spirit, Óðr was said to roam far and wide, seeking knowledge, wisdom, and new experiences. This aspect of his character made him elusive, but it also meant that he was not truly lost but rather distant. In some interpretations, Óðr is seen as a personification of the human soul or the concept of inspiration, which can be fleeting and hard to grasp. These stories offer a more hopeful perspective, suggesting that Óðr's absence was not permanent but rather a temporary separation, and that Freyja's persistent search symbolizes the pursuit of love and enlightenment.

In other versions of the myth, there are hints that Óðr's identity overlaps with that of Odin, the All-Father. The similarities in their names and characteristics have led some scholars to believe that Óðr is another aspect or epithet of Odin himself. If this is the case, Freyja's search for Óðr could represent a deeper, more mystical quest for knowledge and union with the divine.

Throughout her journey, Freyja's actions had a profound impact on the realms she traversed. Her golden tears enriched the earth, leading to the discovery of gold and precious gems by humans and dwarves alike. These treasures became symbols of her love and were often used in rituals and offerings to honor the gods. Additionally, her unwavering devotion and perseverance became legendary, inspiring songs, poems, and stories that were passed down through generations.

Despite the heartache and the relentless passage of time, Freyja's love for Óðr never wavered. She continued her search, knowing that her love was a powerful force that could transcend even the greatest distances. Her journey also led her to experience the vastness of the worlds, deepening her wisdom and compassion for all beings she encountered.

In some versions of the story, Freyja eventually found Óðr, and they were joyously reunited. Their reunion brought immense happiness not only to them but also to the gods and all the realms, as their love was celebrated and revered. In other accounts, Óðr would periodically return to Freyja, only to depart again, perpetuating the cycle of separation and reunion. This cyclical pattern reflects the rhythms of nature and the changing seasons, with Freyja's tears symbolizing the rains that nourish the earth.

Regardless of the ending, the tale of Freyja and Óðr remains a poignant reminder of the complexities of love and the pain of separation. It speaks to the enduring power of devotion and the lengths one will go to for the sake of love. Freyja's relentless quest exemplifies the themes of perseverance, sacrifice, and the transformative power of emotion. Her story continues to resonate, offering insight into the human experience and the universal longing for connection.

The Legacy of the Tale

The story of Freyja's search for Óðr is a testament to the power of love and the resilience of the human (or divine) spirit. It highlights the goddess's strength, not just in her beauty and allure but in her capacity for deep, abiding love. Her journey, marked by golden tears, reflects the bittersweet nature of love—capable of bringing immense joy and profound sorrow.

This tale underscores the belief that love is worth the struggle, that the pain of loss is a reflection of the depth of one's feelings, and that the pursuit of what one holds dear is a noble and courageous endeavor. Freyja's story continues to resonate as a symbol of hope, perseverance, and the unbreakable bond that love can create.

Loki: The Trickster

Loki, the trickster god, is perhaps the most enigmatic and complex figure in Norse mythology. Unlike the other gods who fit neatly into roles of creation, protection, or destruction, Loki defies simple classification. He is a shape-shifter, a master of deceit, and a cunning schemer whose actions bring both aid and calamity to the gods and humans alike. His parentage is unique—born to the giant Fárbauti and the goddess Laufey—placing him between the worlds of the gods (Æsir) and the giants (Jötnar), which contributes to his outsider status among the deities of Asgard.

Loki's stories are a mix of cunning exploits, chaotic endeavors, and unexpected consequences that often serve as catalysts for significant events in Norse lore. His ability to shape-shift is legendary; he transforms into various creatures such as a salmon, a mare, a fly, and even an elderly woman, using these forms to manipulate situations to his advantage. His silver tongue and sharp wit make him both a valuable ally and a dangerous foe. On numerous occasions, Loki's cleverness helps the gods out of tricky situations—like when he orchestrated the building of the walls of Asgard by a giant and then prevented the giant from claiming the sun, the moon, and the goddess Freyja as payment.

He embodies the unpredictable and often destructive force of change, challenging the status quo and bringing both trouble and innovation to the world of the gods. For instance, some of the gods' most treasured possessions, such as Thor's hammer Mjölnir, Odin's spear Gungnir, and Freyja's necklace Brísingamen, are direct results of Loki's misadventures and subsequent attempts to amend them. His actions frequently set off a chain of events that force the gods to react, adapt, and grow, highlighting his role as a catalyst within the divine hierarchy.

The Tragic Tale of Balder's Death

Loki's involvement in the death of Balder, the most beloved of the gods, is one of the most poignant and consequential stories in Norse mythology. Balder, son of Odin and Frigg, was adored by all for his beauty, kindness, and fairness. He began to have ominous dreams foretelling his own death, which greatly alarmed the gods. Seeking to protect her son, Frigg extracted oaths from all things in creation not to harm Balder—stones, metals, plants, animals, and even diseases swore they would not be the cause of his demise.

With Balder seemingly invulnerable, the gods made a game of throwing weapons and objects at him, watching them bounce off harmlessly. Loki, ever the mischief-maker, was displeased by this spectacle and sought to undermine it. Disguising himself as an old woman, he approached Frigg and inquired about the peculiar invincibility of her son. Frigg revealed that she had overlooked one plant—the mistletoe—considering it too young and insignificant to warrant an oath.

Seizing this opportunity, Loki crafted a dart or spear from the mistletoe. During the next gathering where the gods continued their game, Loki approached Balder's blind brother, Hodr. Offering to guide Hodr's hand so he could participate, Loki directed the mistletoe weapon at Balder. The projectile struck Balder, piercing him through, and he fell dead on the spot. The gods were stricken with grief and disbelief; their cherished companion was gone, and the joy of Asgard turned to mourning.

Balder's death was not just a personal loss but a cosmic catastrophe. It marked a turning point in Norse mythology, where the harmony of the gods was shattered, and the shadows of despair and doom loomed large. The sorrow was so profound that the gods sought to bring Balder back from the dead. Odin's son Hermod rode to the underworld on Sleipnir, Odin's eight-legged horse, to plead with Hel, the goddess of the dead, for Balder's return. Hel agreed on one condition: that all things in the world weep for Balder.

Messengers were sent across the realms, and indeed, everything wept—the stones, the trees, the animals, and the people—all except for one giantess named Thökk, who refused to shed a tear. Unbeknownst to the gods, Thökk was Loki in disguise, and her refusal sealed Balder's fate to remain in the underworld until after Ragnarök. This act of treachery deepened the gods' animosity toward Loki and set the stage for his eventual punishment.

In response to his heinous deeds, the gods decided that Loki must be brought to justice. He fled Asgard, hiding in remote mountains and building a house with four doors to watch for approaching enemies. During the day, he transformed himself into a salmon and hid in the nearby river, but the gods eventually discovered his whereabouts. They captured him using a net—an invention Loki himself had created.

As punishment, Loki was bound to three large stones with the entrails of his own son, Narfi, whom he had with his wife Sigyn. Above him, the gods placed a serpent that dripped venom onto his face. Sigyn, ever faithful, stood by his side, catching the venom in a bowl to spare him pain. However, whenever she left to empty the bowl, the venom would drip onto Loki's face, causing him to writhe in agony. His violent thrashing was said to be the cause of earthquakes in the human world.

Loki's binding was meant to last until the onset of Ragnarök, the prophesied end of the world, when he would break free from his bonds. At that time, he would join forces with the giants and lead them against the gods of Asgard in a final, apocalyptic battle. The death of Balder was thus a harbinger of the doom to come—a catalyst that set into motion the events leading to the ultimate destruction and rebirth of the cosmos.

The Duality of Loki's Influence

Loki's actions, while often destructive, also brought about significant changes that were necessary for the evolution of the gods and the world. His role in the myths highlights the belief that chaos and order are intertwined forces, each essential to the other's existence. Without Loki's mischief, many of the gods' greatest treasures and stories would not exist. His presence challenges the gods to adapt and overcome, testing their wisdom, patience, and strength.

Moreover, Loki's complex relationships with other deities add depth to his character. He is a blood brother to Odin, which grants him a certain level of acceptance among the Æsir, despite his Jötunn heritage and his tendency to cause trouble. His interactions with Thor often oscillate between cooperation and conflict. In some tales, they embark on adventures together, like retrieving Thor's stolen hammer from the giant Thrym—a feat accomplished through cunning and disguise. In others, Loki's actions directly oppose Thor's interests, contributing to the layered dynamics of their relationship.

Loki's Legacy and the Reflection of Norse Values

Loki embodies the unpredictable aspects of existence—the sudden changes, the unforeseen consequences, and the delicate balance between creation and destruction. His stories serve as cautionary tales about the repercussions of deceit, the complexities of fate, and the inevitable interplay between good and evil. Through Loki, the Norse myths explore the idea that even the gods are not immune to folly and that wisdom often comes through hardship and loss.

The tale of Balder's death, in particular, reflects the Norse understanding of fate (or "wyrd") and the concept that some events are predestined, beyond the control of even the most powerful beings. It also underscores the themes of sacrifice and the transient nature of life and happiness.

Modern Interpretations and Enduring Fascination

In contemporary times, Loki continues to captivate the imagination. His character has been reinterpreted in novels, films, television shows, and comics, often highlighting his trickster qualities while delving deeper into his psyche. These modern portrayals explore his motivations, inner conflicts, and the circumstances that shape his actions, presenting him as a more nuanced and sometimes sympathetic figure.

Loki's enduring appeal lies in his complexity and the timeless themes his stories convey. He represents the multifaceted nature of individuals—the capacity for both good and ill within the same being. His tales invite reflection on personal responsibility, the consequences of one's choices, and the inevitable changes that life brings.

Conclusion

Loki remains one of the most intriguing figures in Norse mythology—a symbol of chaos, change, and the intricate dance between order and disorder. His involvement in the death of Balder and the subsequent events leading to Ragnarök highlight his central role in the Norse cosmic narrative. Through his stories, we gain insight into the values, beliefs, and philosophical contemplations of the Norse people, as well as a deeper understanding of the complexities inherent in all stories of gods and men.

Chapter 2:
The Legend of Loki

Loki's legacy extends through his remarkable and fearsome children, each embodying elements of chaos, destruction, and foreboding that mirror their father's complex and enigmatic nature. Among his offspring with the giantess Angrboða—whose name means "Anguish-boding" or "She Who

Brings Grief"—are three of the most notorious and significant beings in Norse mythology: Hel, the ruler of the underworld; Jörmungandr, the colossal Midgard Serpent; and Fenrir, the monstrous wolf destined to play a pivotal role in the cosmos's fate. These children are not only significant figures in their own right but also pivotal players in the prophesied events of Ragnarök, the cataclysmic end of the world.

Loki himself is a complex deity—neither entirely benevolent nor malevolent—whose actions often bring about significant consequences for both gods and humans. His progeny amplify his role as an agent of chaos and catalyst for change, serving as instruments through which the prophesied destruction and subsequent rebirth of the world are fulfilled.

During Ragnarök, the roles of Loki's children are central to the unfolding apocalypse:

Hel unleashes the dead to join the forces against the gods, tipping the scales in the colossal battles.

Jörmungandr emerges from the ocean, causing massive floods and confronting Thor in their final duel.

Fenrir breaks free from his bindings, his massive jaws stretching from the earth to the sky, consuming everything in his path, including Odin himself.

These events underscore the Norse belief in an inexorable fate that even the gods cannot escape. The destruction wrought by Loki's children is not viewed solely as an end but also as a necessary precursor to renewal. After Ragnarök, the world is expected to rise anew from the seas, purified and ready for a fresh beginning, with surviving gods and two human beings—Líf and Lífþrasir—to repopulate and restore balance.

Loki's relationships with his children further illustrate his multifaceted character. While he is often seen as a trickster and instigator of discord, his paternal connections add depth to his narrative. His attempts to protect his children from the gods' fears and subsequent actions against them can be interpreted as a reflection of familial bonds and the complexities within them.

In exploring the tales of Loki's children, one delves into the rich tapestry of Norse mythology, where gods and giants, order and chaos, life and death are in constant interplay. The stories serve as metaphors for natural phenomena and human experiences, reflecting the Norse people's understanding of the world's unpredictability and the cycles that govern existence.

The legacy of Loki and his progeny continues to captivate modern imagination, influencing literature, art, and popular culture. Their narratives offer timeless insights into the human condition, the inevitability of change, and the enduring hope for renewal amidst destruction. By examining the roles and significance of Hel, Jörmungandr, and Fenrir, we gain a deeper appreciation for the complexity and depth of Norse mythology and its enduring relevance across the ages.

Hel

Hel: The Enigmatic Goddess of the Underworld in Norse Mythology

Hel, the goddess of the underworld, is one of the most compelling and complex figures in Norse mythology, embodying the profound dichotomy of life and death. As the daughter of Loki, the infamous trickster god known for his cunning and shape-shifting abilities, and the giantess Angrboða—whose name means "the bringer of grief"—Hel's lineage is a fusion of divine mischief and the primordial forces of the giants. Born in the shadowy realms of Jotunheim, the land of the giants, Hel's very existence is a testament to the intricate and often tumultuous relationships among gods, giants, and other beings in Norse cosmology.

The Dual Nature of Hel

From the moment of her birth, Hel was marked by a striking and unsettling duality. Her appearance reflects her unique nature: one-half of her body is that of a living, vibrant woman—radiant, healthy, and beautiful—representing life, vitality, and the allure of existence. The other half is that of a corpse—darkened, decayed, and grim—symbolizing death, decay, and the inevitable end that awaits all living beings. This physical manifestation of life and death coexisting within a single entity makes Hel a powerful symbol of the natural cycle and the fine line between existence and oblivion.

Her visage was so disturbing that even the gods found it unsettling. Yet, it also commanded a certain respect, for she embodied truths that none could escape. Hel's duality extends beyond her physical appearance; it permeates her personality and role within the mythological narrative. She is both compassionate and unyielding, offering a realm for the dead while also enforcing the inexorable laws of mortality.

The Banishment to Helheim

The Aesir, the pantheon of Norse gods residing in Asgard, became aware of Hel and her siblings—Jörmungandr, the Midgard Serpent, and Fenrir, the monstrous wolf—all children of Loki and Angrboða. Prophecies foretold that these offspring would bring great misfortune and challenges to the gods. Seeking to prevent these dire outcomes, Odin, the All-Father and ruler of the Aesir, took action to manage the potential threats posed by Loki's children.

Odin cast Hel into the deepest, darkest region of the underworld, granting her dominion over the nine realms of the dead who die not in battle but of sickness, old age, or misfortune. This realm came to be known as Helheim—literally "house of Hel"—a cold and shadowy place far removed from the vibrancy of the living world and the glory of Valhalla, where warriors slain heroically in battle were welcomed.

Hel's banishment was not merely an act of rejection but also one of necessity and balance. By assigning her this role, Odin acknowledged the essential function she would serve in the cosmic order. Hel accepted her fate, establishing her sovereignty over Helheim and becoming a pivotal figure in the management of souls and the afterlife.

The Realm of Helheim

Helheim is depicted as a vast, desolate land enveloped in perpetual gloom and chill. It lies beneath one of the roots of Yggdrasil, the World Tree, anchoring it to the darker aspects of existence. Surrounded by high walls and a massive gate called Eljúdnir ("Sleet Cold"), Helheim is guarded against escape and intrusion, emphasizing the finality of death.

Within this realm, Hel presides from her hall, also named Eljúdnir, which is described as imposing and grim. The hall's furnishings and surroundings reflect the somber nature of her domain. Her table is Hunger, her knife is Famine, her bed is Sickbed, and the curtains around it are Blighted Misfortune. These symbolic elements reinforce the themes of deprivation and the stark realities of mortality.

Hel's servants, Ganglati and Ganglöt, move with extreme slowness, symbolizing the lethargy and stagnation associated with death. The river Gjöll, meaning "noisy," flows near Helheim, crossed by the Gjallarbrú, a bridge that all souls must traverse, guarded by the maiden Modgud.

Unlike the fiery torment of the Christian concept of Hell, Helheim is not necessarily a place of punishment but rather one of somber existence. Souls dwell here in a shadowy reflection of their former lives, experiencing neither the joys of Valhalla nor the tortures of a punitive afterlife. It is a realm of rest, introspection, and perhaps melancholy, reflecting the Norse acceptance of death as a natural, if somber, part of life.

The Duality of Hel's Role

Hel's dominion over the dead underscores her vital role in maintaining the balance of the cosmos. She is the custodian of souls who did not die gloriously in battle—those who passed away from illness, age, or accidents. In a culture that highly valued heroism and martial prowess, Hel provided a necessary counterpart, ensuring that all souls had a place in the afterlife regardless of their earthly deeds.

Her impartiality in overseeing the dead reflects the inevitable and unbiased nature of death itself. Hel does not discriminate or pass judgment based on one's status or actions in life. Instead, she offers a final abode where souls can reside, underscoring the Norse belief in the inescapable fate that binds all beings.

Despite her grim associations, Hel is not portrayed as inherently malevolent. She exhibits a certain dignity and adherence to the rules that govern her realm. Her interactions with other gods and beings demonstrate her authority and the respect she commands within the mythological hierarchy.

Hel's Place in the Myths

Hel features prominently in several Norse myths, most notably in the tale of the death of Balder, the god of light, joy, and purity. Balder's death is one of the most tragic events in Norse mythology and serves as a precursor to Ragnarök, the end of the world.

When Balder is killed—unintentionally by his blind brother Hodr, manipulated by Loki—the gods are devastated. His spirit descends to

33

Helheim, and the gods desperately seek to bring him back to Asgard. Hermod, another son of Odin, rides to Helheim on Odin's eight-legged horse Sleipnir to plead with Hel for Balder's release.

Hel agrees to release Balder on one condition: that all things in the world, living and non-living, weep for him to prove that he is truly beloved. The gods traverse the realms, and indeed, all weep for Balder except for a giantess named Thokk, widely believed to be Loki in disguise. Thokk's refusal seals Balder's fate, and he remains in Helheim until after Ragnarök.

This story highlights Hel's adherence to the rules and the limits of her compassion. She offers a chance for Balder's resurrection but maintains the conditions that uphold the cosmic balance. Her role in this myth underscores the finality of death and the idea that even the gods are subject to the immutable laws of fate.

Symbolism and Interpretation

Hel embodies the Norse understanding of death as an integral part of the natural order. Her dual appearance symbolizes the interconnectedness of life and death—the beauty of existence and the decay that follows. She represents the acceptance of mortality and the notion that death is not an adversary but a necessary transition to another state of being.

In a broader sense, Hel reflects the themes of balance and duality prevalent in Norse cosmology. Just as day balances night, and order balances chaos, Hel's presence ensures that the cycle of life is complete. Her realm provides a counterpoint to the glory and honor of Valhalla, reminding mortals and gods alike that not all paths lead to fame and that every life, regardless of its deeds, has value and a place in the cosmic scheme.

Cultural Significance and Legacy

Hel's character offers deep insights into the Norse psyche and cultural values. Her portrayal is neither wholly negative nor entirely positive but nuanced, capturing the complexity of death's role in human experience. She serves as a figure of solemn respect rather than fear, embodying the inevitability that all must face.

The concept of Hel and her realm may have influenced later interpretations of the underworld in other cultures and religions. The name "Hel" itself is cognate with the Old English "hell," though the Norse Helheim is distinct from the Christian Hell in both function and philosophy.

In modern times, Hel continues to fascinate scholars, artists, and enthusiasts of mythology. She appears in various adaptations of Norse myths in literature, film, and other media, often explored as a character of depth and intrigue. Her story invites contemplation of mortality, the afterlife, and the acceptance of life's transient nature.

Conclusion

Hel, the goddess of the underworld, is one of Norse mythology's most enigmatic and significant deities. Her unique duality, authoritative role, and essential function in the cosmic balance make her a compelling figure. Through her, the Norse myths convey profound truths about life, death, and the cycles that govern existence.

Hel's legacy is solemn respect and acceptance, reminding us of the transient nature of life and the universal journey toward the unknown. She personifies the inevitable fate that unites all beings, offering a realm where souls find their final resting place. In embracing both the beauty and decay inherent in existence, Hel embodies the complex interplay of forces that shape the world, inviting reflection on the mysteries that lie beyond the mortal realm.

Jormungandr - The Origins and Encirclement of Midgard

The Birth and Early Life of Jormungandr

Jormungandr's story begins with his birth—a momentous event that set the stage for his crucial role in Norse mythology. He is one of the three monstrous children born to Loki and the giantess Angrboða, whose name means "the bringer of grief." His siblings are Fenrir, the colossal wolf destined to slay Odin during Ragnarok, and Hel, the ruler of the underworld. The birth of these fearsome offspring alarmed the gods, who foresaw the potential threat they posed to the cosmic order.

From a young age, Jormungandr's tremendous growth was evident. His size and strength increased at an unprecedented rate, and the gods quickly recognized the danger he represented. Odin, the All-Father and ruler of the Aesir gods, sought to mitigate this threat. In an effort to prevent the ominous prophecies from coming true, Odin decided to remove Loki's children from the realms where they could cause harm. He cast Jormungandr into the great ocean that encircles Midgard, the world of humans.

In the depths of the ocean, Jormungandr continued to grow until he became so immense that he could encircle the entire world, grasping his own tail in his mouth. This act of encircling Midgard forms a powerful symbol known as the ouroboros, representing the eternal cycle of destruction and rebirth. The image of the serpent biting its own tail is a motif found in various cultures, symbolizing infinity, unity, and the cyclical nature of the universe. In Jormungandr's case, it signifies the interconnectedness of all things and the delicate balance that maintains the world's stability.

Symbolism of the Ouroboros and Jormungandr's Presence

Jormungandr's presence in the ocean symbolizes the vast, unknown, and potentially dangerous forces that lie beyond the safety of the known world. The ocean, in Norse cosmology, represents the chaotic and untamed aspects of nature. The serpent's encirclement of Midgard serves as both a protective boundary and a looming threat, emphasizing the precariousness of existence and the thin line between order and chaos.

His existence is a constant reminder of the hidden threats lurking just beyond the horizon. The tension of Jormungandr holding his tail in his mouth represents a delicate balance. Should he ever release his tail, it would signal the beginning of the end times—Ragnarok. This symbolism underscores the Norse belief in the inevitable cycles of destruction and renewal that govern the cosmos.

The Role of Jormungandr in Norse Mythology

Jormungandr is not merely a passive creature residing in the ocean's depths. His very existence is intricately tied to the fate of the world and the gods. The Midgard Serpent is said to cause the ocean's tides by the movement of his massive coils, affecting the lives of those who dwell on land and sea alike. His immense size and power make him a formidable force that even the gods approach with caution.

In the myths, Jormungandr harbors a deep enmity towards Thor, the god of thunder and protector of humanity. This animosity is highlighted in several tales, showcasing the ongoing struggle between these two powerful beings.

One of the most famous stories involves Thor's fishing expedition with the giant Hymir. Disguised as a young man, Thor accompanies Hymir on a boat trip into the open sea, determined to confront the serpent. Using an ox head as bait—a sizable lure for a creature of immense proportions—Thor casts his line into the ocean. Jormungandr takes the bait, and a tremendous struggle ensues as Thor attempts to pull the serpent to the surface.

As Thor prepares to strike Jormungandr with his mighty hammer Mjölnir, Hymir, terrified of the catastrophic consequences that might follow, cuts the fishing line. The serpent sinks back into the depths, and Thor is left enraged at the lost opportunity. This encounter not only showcases the might of both Thor and Jormungandr but also foreshadows their final, cataclysmic confrontation during Ragnarok.

Another tale from the Prose Edda recounts Thor's visit to the realm of Útgarða-Loki, a powerful giant and master of illusions. As part of a series of challenges designed to humiliate Thor and his companions, Thor is asked to lift a large cat as a test of strength. Despite his immense power, Thor can only manage to raise one of the cat's paws off the ground. Later, it is revealed that the cat was actually Jormungandr in disguise, and Thor's partial success is seen as a remarkable feat, given the serpent's colossal size.

The Prophecy of Ragnarok

Jormungandr's most significant role comes at the end of times, during Ragnarok, the prophesied apocalypse in Norse mythology. According to the seeress's prophecy in the poem "Völuspá", Ragnarok will be heralded by a series of cataclysmic events. One of the signs is the great serpent releasing his tail and rising from the ocean depths, causing massive tidal waves and poisoning the sky with his venom. The land will tremble, the seas will surge, and the skies will darken as Jormungandr emerges, ready to play his part in the final battle.

During Ragnarok, Jormungandr will face his arch-nemesis, Thor, in an epic and fated duel. The two are destined to slay each other, fulfilling the ominous prophecies that have loomed over their existences. The battlefield becomes a scene of unparalleled destruction as they engage in combat. Thor, wielding Mjölnir, strikes powerful blows against the serpent, while Jormungandr retaliates with venomous attacks and crushing coils.

Ultimately, Thor succeeds in defeating the serpent, striking him down with a final, mighty blow. However, Thor manages to take only nine steps before succumbing to the deadly venom that Jormungandr spews forth in his death throes. This mutual destruction underscores the inevitability of the cosmic cycle and the perpetual struggle between order and chaos. Their deaths symbolize the end of an era and pave the way for the rebirth of the world.

Symbolism and Legacy

Jormungandr embodies the themes of cyclical conflict and the delicate balance between creation and destruction. As the ouroboros, he represents the eternal cycle of life, death, and rebirth—a fundamental concept in many mythologies and philosophies. His continuous encirclement of Midgard signifies the world's ongoing processes and the interconnectedness of all existence.

His battle with Thor, a god of order and protection, symbolizes the ultimate clash between chaotic forces and the stabilizing powers of the cosmos. Thor's role as the defender of both gods and humans against giants and monstrous beings highlights the perpetual effort to maintain balance and harmony in the face of overwhelming odds.

The Midgard Serpent's story is a reminder of the fragile nature of existence and the constant presence of potential threats. It reflects the Norse understanding of the world as a place of inherent struggle, where even the gods are not immune to the forces of chaos and fate. The tales emphasize that conflict and adversity are integral parts of the cosmic order, and that from destruction, new beginnings can emerge.

Jormungandr's tale, with its powerful imagery and profound themes, continues to resonate as a symbol of the inevitable cycles that govern the universe. His presence in Norse mythology has influenced various aspects of culture and art throughout history.

In ancient times, the image of the serpent biting its tail appeared on runestones and amulets, symbolizing protection and the eternal nature of life. The ouroboros motif, associated with Jormungandr, has been adopted in various philosophical and spiritual contexts beyond Norse culture, representing concepts such as infinity, unity, and the cyclical nature of time.

In modern literature, Jormungandr has been featured in novels, poems, and scholarly works exploring Norse myths and their relevance to contemporary themes. His character often serves as a metaphor for the challenges humanity faces against overwhelming and uncontrollable forces.

In popular culture, Jormungandr appears in video games, films, and television series, often depicted as a colossal and awe-inspiring creature. These portrayals introduce the Midgard Serpent to new audiences, highlighting the enduring fascination with Norse mythology and its rich tapestry of gods, monsters, and cosmic events.

In the end, Jormungandr's legacy is one of awe and respect. He embodies the vastness and mystery of the cosmos, the inevitability of change, and the ultimate reconciliation of opposing forces. His role in Norse mythology highlights the complexities of the universe and the understanding that balance is maintained through the interplay of contradictory elements.

Jormungandr's presence in the Norse pantheon serves as a powerful reminder of the interconnectedness of all things. His story encourages reflection on the cyclical patterns that govern life and the acceptance of change as a fundamental aspect of existence. The eternal dance of creation and destruction that he symbolizes continues to captivate and inspire, offering insights into the enduring mysteries that shape the world.

By exploring Jormungandr's tale, we gain a deeper appreciation for the Norse worldview—a perspective that embraces the complexities of fate, the inevitability of change, and the profound connections between all elements of the cosmos. His story is not just a myth but a timeless reflection on the human condition and the forces that influence our journey through life.

Fenrir

Fenrir, the great wolf and one of the children of Loki and the giantess Angrboda, stands as one of the most terrifying figures in Norse mythology. His immense strength and fierce nature make him a symbol of the uncontrollable forces of chaos and destruction. The story of Fenrir not only emphasizes the constant tension between order and chaos but also reflects the inevitability of fate and the cyclical nature of the cosmos.

The Growing Threat

From the moment of his birth, Fenrir's potential for destruction was evident. As he grew at an alarming rate, the gods became increasingly concerned about the danger he posed. Fenrir's strength was unparalleled, and his hunger for power and freedom made him a threat not only to the gods but also to the very fabric of the universe.

The gods, foreseeing the devastation Fenrir could unleash, decided to bind him in order to neutralize the threat. However, Fenrir's strength was such that he easily broke free from the first two chains they attempted to bind him with. Realizing that ordinary means would not suffice, the gods turned to the dwarves, master craftsmen and enchanters, to forge a magical chain capable of restraining the mighty wolf.

The dwarves created a chain called Gleipnir, crafted from six impossible ingredients: the sound of a cat's footfall, the beard of a woman, the roots of a mountain, the sinews of a bear, the breath of a fish, and the spittle of a bird. Despite its delicate appearance, Gleipnir was imbued with powerful magic, rendering it unbreakable.

The gods, under the guise of a test of strength, coaxed Fenrir into allowing them to bind him with Gleipnir. Fenrir, suspicious of the gods' intentions, agreed to the test only if one of the gods would place a hand in his mouth as a pledge of good faith. The god Tyr, known for his bravery, volunteered, understanding the risk involved. As the chain tightened and Fenrir realized he could not break free, he bit off Tyr's hand in rage, a permanent reminder of the gods' deception.

Bound by Gleipnir, Fenrir was left on the island of Lyngvi, where he would remain until Ragnarok. Despite being restrained, Fenrir's presence continued to loom large over the cosmos, symbolizing the latent chaos and destruction that even the gods could not entirely control.

The Norse seers prophesied that during Ragnarok, the end of the world, Fenrir would break free from his chains. This cataclysmic event would be marked by the wolf's escape and his subsequent actions. The prophecy foretold that Fenrir would cause immense devastation, with his gaping maw so vast that his lower jaw would touch the earth while his upper jaw reached the sky. As he rampaged through the realms, Fenrir would devour Odin, the All-Father and king of the gods, in a moment of ultimate chaos and destruction.

However, Odin's death would not go unavenged. Vidar, one of Odin's sons, was destined to confront Fenrir. In a climactic battle, Vidar would slay the monstrous wolf by tearing apart his jaws, using a special shoe crafted from all the leather scraps saved by cobblers. Vidar's victory, while avenging his father's death, also symbolizes the resilience of order and the hope for renewal amidst the chaos of Ragnarok.

Symbolism and Legacy

Fenrir's story is rich with symbolism. As a creature of chaos, he embodies the uncontrollable and destructive aspects of nature and the universe. His immense power and eventual release during Ragnarok serve as a reminder of the fragility of order and the ever-present potential for chaos to erupt and overturn the established balance.

The binding of Fenrir represents the gods' attempt to impose order on chaos, an endeavor that is ultimately temporary. The breaking of Gleipnir and Fenrir's actions during Ragnarok underscore the inevitability of change and the cyclical nature of existence, where creation and destruction are inextricably linked.

Fenrir's tale also highlights themes of fate and destiny, central elements in Norse mythology. The gods' knowledge of the prophecy did not prevent its fulfillment, illustrating the concept that some events are predestined and unavoidable, regardless of the measures taken to prevent them.

Summary

Fenrir, as the monstrous wolf and child of Loki, remains one of the most powerful and fearsome figures in Norse mythology. His story is a poignant reminder of the constant struggle to maintain balance in the universe, the limits of control over chaotic forces, and the inexorable march of fate. The tale of Fenrir's rise and the havoc he will wreak during Ragnarok encapsulates the Norse view of the cosmos as a place where order and chaos are in a perpetual dance, with each cycle leading to renewal and rebirth.

These children play pivotal roles in the prophesied events of Ragnarok, each embodying aspects of their father's chaotic influence and highlighting the interconnectedness of their fates with the gods. Their existence and actions serve as a testament to the far-reaching impact of Loki's legacy, demonstrating how his influence extends beyond his own deeds to shape the very destiny of the world. Through their stories, we explore themes of inevitability, the cyclical nature of time, and the profound consequences of chaos unleashed.

Ragnarok: The Final Act

Loki's role in Ragnarok, the end of the world, cements his position as an agent of chaos. Unbound during the final battle, Loki leads the forces of the giants and the dead against the gods of Asgard. This apocalyptic event marks the ultimate confrontation between the forces of chaos and order, a theme central to Norse mythology. Loki's alliance with the giants and his orchestration of the assault on Asgard highlight his transformative and disruptive influence on the cosmos.

In the climactic moments of Ragnarok, Loki faces Heimdall, the watchman of the gods. Heimdall, known for his keen senses and vigilance, stands as the guardian of the Bifrost bridge, which connects Asgard to the other realms. The confrontation between Loki and Heimdall is fierce and relentless, embodying the cosmic struggle between chaos and order. Their battle results in mutual destruction, symbolizing the cataclysmic clash that brings about the end of the current world order.

Ragnarok is not merely an end but a transformation, a theme resonant throughout Loki's tales. The destruction and death that occur during this final battle pave the way for renewal and rebirth. As the old world is consumed by fire and flood, a new world emerges from the devastation, reflecting the cyclical nature of existence. This process of destruction and regeneration is a fundamental aspect of Norse cosmology, illustrating the perpetual cycle of creation, destruction, and rebirth.

Loki's actions, though often destructive, are integral to the cosmic balance. His role in Ragnarok underscores his function as both a catalyst for change and a harbinger of chaos. Through his deeds, Loki disrupts the existing order, but this disruption is necessary for the eventual renewal of the world. In this way, Loki's legacy is one of paradox and duality; he is both the destroyer and the instigator of new beginnings.

We have delved into the tales of Loki, so now reflect on the dualities within your own life and the world around you. Consider how chaos and order, creation and destruction, are intertwined. Loki's stories, with their intricate blend of mischief and redemption, mirror the complexities of human existence, where moments of chaos often lead to unexpected growth and transformation. By exploring these myths, we gain insight into the delicate balance that shapes our lives and the universe.

Let Loki's stories inspire you to embrace the complexities of life and to see the value in both the light and the shadows. His dual nature teaches us that understanding and integrating both aspects of our character can lead to a more profound comprehension of ourselves and our place in the world. The trickster god's tales encourage us to acknowledge our own imperfections and the unpredictability of life, finding strength in our resilience and adaptability.

Continue this journey with an open mind, ready to uncover the lessons hidden within the myths of the trickster god. As we navigate through Loki's adventures and misadventures, we are reminded that wisdom often comes from unexpected places and that the path to enlightenment is rarely straightforward. Embrace the stories of Loki as a guide to understanding the intricacies of human nature and the ever-present dance between chaos and order, and let these ancient tales enrich your perspective on life's many dualities.

Chapter 3:

Heroes of Midgard

Journey to Midgard, the realm of humans in Norse cosmology.

Midgard is a world suspended between Asgard's divine realms and the underworld's chaotic depths. It is encircled by the vast serpent Jörmungandr, the Midgard Serpent, whose presence symbolizes the boundaries of the known world. This land is brimming with peril and possibility, a place where the ordinary and the supernatural intersect and where heroes rise to confront external threats and their destinies.

Here, legendary figures like Sigurd and Beowulf carve their names into history through acts of unparalleled bravery and adventure. Sigurd, one of the most celebrated heroes in Norse mythology, is famed for slaying the dragon Fafnir. Armed with the sword Gram, forged by the master smith Regin, Sigurd begins a quest that tests his courage, wisdom, and integrity. His victory over Fafnir grants him not only immense treasure but also a deep understanding of the world's hidden knowledge as he gains the ability to understand the language of birds. However, his journey is fraught with betrayal and tragedy, particularly in his relationships with Brynhildr, the valkyrie, and Gudrun, his wife, highlighting the complex interplay of fate and free will.

Beowulf, while rooted in Old English literature, shares strong ties with Norse heroic tradition. As a warrior of the Geats, he comes to the aid of King Hrothgar of the Danes, whose hall is terrorized by the monstrous Grendel. Beowulf's battles against Grendel, Grendel's vengeful mother, and later, a fearsome dragon, showcase his superhuman strength and unwavering courage. His story reflects themes of honor, loyalty, and the hero's duty to protect others, even at great personal cost. Beowulf's final act of slaying the dragon, which leads to his own death, epitomizes the ultimate sacrifice a hero makes for the safety of his people.

Midgard serves as the heart of human experience in Norse cosmology—a realm where mortals live their lives under the watchful eyes of the gods yet are free to make choices that shape their destinies. The challenges faced by heroes like Sigurd and Beowulf are emblematic of the human condition, reflecting the Norse belief in a world governed by both fate and personal valor. The landscape of Midgard is dotted with mysterious forests, treacherous mountains, and uncharted seas, each harboring creatures like trolls, giants, and dragons that test the mettle of those who dare to confront them.

The tales of these heroes are rich with themes of valor, resilience, and the timeless struggle between good and evil. They delve into the complexities of honor, the consequences of pride, and the inevitability of death. The stories embody the essence of the hero's journey in Norse mythology, where the protagonist often undergoes a profound transformation through trials and tribulations. These narratives emphasize that true heroism lies not just in physical strength but also in wisdom, humility, and the willingness to face one's own flaws.

Moreover, the legends underscore the Norse concept of fate—known as wyrd—and how it intertwines with personal choice. While the heroes are often destined for greatness, their paths are not without hardship or sorrow. Sigurd's tragic end and Beowulf's mortal wound from the dragon serve as reminders of the transient nature of life and glory. Yet, their legacies endure, immortalized in the sagas and songs passed down through generations.

Midgard's portrayal in these stories offers a window into the values and ideals of Viking society. The emphasis on courage, loyalty, and reputation reflects a culture that esteemed warriors and revered the bonds of kinship and honor. The heroes' interactions with divine beings, magical artifacts, and mythical creatures highlight a worldview where the sacred and the mundane coexist and where individuals' actions can have far-reaching effects on both their world and the realms beyond.

In exploring Midgard and the sagas of its heroes, we gain insight into the Norse psyche—a people who navigated a harsh and unpredictable world with stoicism and a fierce sense of purpose. The enduring popularity of these tales speaks to their universal themes and the profound human truths they convey. They invite us to reflect on our own journeys, the challenges we face, and the legacies we wish to leave behind.

The legends of Sigurd, Beowulf, and other heroes of Midgard continue to resonate today, inspiring countless retellings in literature, art, and popular culture. They remind us of the timeless allure of the hero's journey—a path of adventure, self-discovery, and the quest to overcome the forces that threaten to engulf us. In the realm of Midgard, the echoes of these epic tales persist, inviting each new generation to embark on their own heroic quests amidst the perils and possibilities of the human experience.

The Birth and Early Life of Sigurd

Sigurd was born into a noble lineage, the son of Sigmund, a great warrior, and Hjordis. However, his early life was marked by tragedy, as his father was slain in battle before his birth. Raised by his mother and the dwarf smith Regin, Sigurd grew up unaware of his illustrious heritage. Regin, who was both his foster father and mentor, played a crucial role in shaping Sigurd's destiny.

Regin was not just a skilled smith; he harbored a deep grudge against his brother, Fafnir. Once a dwarf, Fafnir had transformed into a monstrous dragon after greedily hoarding a cursed treasure, including the powerful ring Andvaranaut. Regin sought revenge and saw in Sigurd a means to achieve it.

To prepare Sigurd for the daunting task of slaying Fafnir, Regin forged for him a magnificent sword called Gram. The sword was no ordinary weapon; it was crafted from the fragments of Sigmund's broken sword and possessed unparalleled sharpness and strength. With Gram in hand, Sigurd was destined for greatness.

Under Regin's guidance, Sigurd set out to confront Fafnir, who dwelt in the wilderness guarding his immense hoard of treasure. The journey was perilous, filled with challenges and dangers. Upon reaching the lair of the dragon, Sigurd displayed both courage and cunning. Following Odin's advice, who had appeared to him in disguise, Sigurd dug a trench and concealed himself within it. As Fafnir slithered over the trench, Sigurd plunged Gram into the dragon's heart, delivering a fatal blow.

As Fafnir lay dying, he warned Sigurd of the curse upon the treasure, a curse that would bring misfortune and death to those who possessed it. Nevertheless, Sigurd took the treasure, including the cursed ring Andvaranaut, ignoring the dragon's ominous prophecy.

After slaying Fafnir, Sigurd confronted Regin, who had secretly plotted to kill him and take the treasure for himself. Realizing Regin's treachery, Sigurd killed him, thereby securing the treasure for himself. Following this, he cooked and ate a portion of Fafnir's heart, which granted him the ability to understand the language of birds. The birds warned him of Regin's intentions, confirming his suspicions.

Sigurd's acquisition of the treasure and the ring marked the beginning of a series of dramatic events. The curse of the treasure loomed large, casting a shadow over his life. Despite the curse, Sigurd's heroic deeds and bravery earned him widespread renown. He became a symbol of the ideal hero, celebrated for his strength, courage, and determination.

The Legacy of Sigurd

Sigurd's story does not end with the slaying of Fafnir. His adventures continued, filled with romance, betrayal, and tragedy. He became entangled in the complex politics of royal courts and the legendary tale of the Nibelungs. His love story with the Valkyrie Brynhild and his tragic death at the hands of treachery are key elements in the greater epic known as the "Volsunga Saga."

The tale of Sigurd and the dragon Fafnir has been immortalized in various forms of literature and art, most notably in the medieval German epic "Nibelungenlied" and Richard Wagner's opera cycle "Der Ring des Nibelungen." The story serves as a powerful narrative about the hero's journey, the corrupting influence of greed, and the inevitable nature of fate.

The story of Sigurd and Fafnir is rich with symbolism. The dragon, often seen as a guardian of treasures and a symbol of chaos, represents the ultimate challenge for the hero. The cursed treasure symbolizes greed's destructive nature and fate's inevitability. Sigurd's heroism, his victory over the dragon, and his tragic end highlight the complex interplay of human virtues and flaws.

Sigurd's saga is a testament to the timeless appeal of the hero's journey. It explores the pursuit of glory, ambition's consequences, and legends' enduring nature. As one of the greatest heroes in Norse mythology, Sigurd's legacy continues to inspire and captivate audiences, serving as a reminder of the power and perils of heroic quests.

Beowulf

The epic tale of Beowulf, the quintessential Anglo-Saxon hero, is a story rich with themes of bravery, sacrifice, and the hero's unwavering duty to protect others. Beowulf's journey mirrors the archetypal Norse hero, characterized by epic battles, monstrous adversaries, and an enduring legacy. His story unfolds in three main episodes, each highlighting his heroic nature and the values of the culture from which the epic originates.

The Journey to the Danes and the Battle with Grendel

The story begins with Beowulf, a Geatish warrior of great strength and noble lineage, hearing of the plight of the Danish king Hrothgar. The kingdom of the Danes is terrorized by Grendel, a monstrous creature who invades the mead hall of Heorot every night, killing Hrothgar's warriors and sowing fear among the people. Determined to prove his valor and repay a debt of honor to Hrothgar, who had once helped his father, Beowulf sails to Denmark with a band of loyal warriors.

Upon his arrival, Beowulf boldly declares his intention to face Grendel without weapons, relying solely on his immense strength and courage. That night, as Grendel attacks Heorot, Beowulf confronts him. A fierce struggle ensues, showcasing Beowulf's unmatched bravery and prowess. In a dramatic display of strength, Beowulf grips Grendel's arm with such force that he tears it from the monster's body. Mortally wounded, Grendel flees into the wilderness, where he eventually dies from his injuries. The Danes rejoice, and Beowulf is hailed as a hero, celebrated for his incredible feat.

However, the danger is not yet over. Grendel's mother, a fearsome and vengeful creature, emerges from her underwater lair to avenge her son's death. She attacks Heorot, killing one of Hrothgar's trusted advisors and retreating with his body. Grieving and desperate, Hrothgar appeals to Beowulf once more.

Beowulf accepts the challenge and descends into the murky waters of the mere, where Grendel's mother resides. Armed with a sword borrowed from Hrothgar, Beowulf battles the formidable creature in her underwater lair. The sword proves ineffective against her tough hide, and the situation becomes dire. However, Beowulf spots a massive, ancient sword hanging on the wall of the lair, a weapon forged by giants. With this sword, he decapitates Grendel's mother, ending her reign of terror. He also finds Grendel's corpse and beheads it, bringing the monster's head back to Hrothgar as a trophy and proof of his victory.

Beowulf returns to Geatland, where he eventually becomes king. He rules wisely and peacefully for fifty years, earning the love and respect of his people. However, his final challenge comes when a dragon, angered by the theft of a precious cup from its hoard, begins ravaging the land. Despite his advanced age, Beowulf resolves to face the dragon, knowing that it is his duty to protect his kingdom, even at the cost of his own life.

Beowulf, accompanied by a small group of warriors, confronts the dragon. In the ensuing battle, his men are overwhelmed by fear and flee, leaving only his loyal kinsman Wiglaf to stand by his side. Beowulf fights valiantly but is mortally wounded by the dragon's fiery breath. With Wiglaf's help, he delivers the final blow, slaying the dragon. However, the victory comes at a great cost; Beowulf succumbs to his wounds, dying a hero's death.

The Legacy of Beowulf

Beowulf's story is a testament to the heroic ideal in Anglo-Saxon and Norse cultures. His bravery, strength, and willingness to face death for the greater good embody the values of the warrior ethos. The epic highlights the transient nature of life and the importance of leaving behind a legacy of courage and honor.

In his final moments, Beowulf expresses concern for his people's future, demonstrating his selfless nature and the responsibility he feels as a leader. His death is a profound loss, mourned by his people, who honor him with a magnificent funeral and burial mound. The dragon's hoard is buried with him, symbolizing the futility of wealth and the enduring value of heroism and sacrifice.

Beowulf's tale resonates as a powerful narrative of the hero's journey, illustrating the timeless themes of bravery, loyalty, and the ultimate sacrifice. It stands as a monument to the human spirit's capacity to confront and overcome the darkest forces, both external and internal, in the pursuit of a greater good.

We have delved into their stories and witnessed the valor and resilience that define the hero's journey in Norse mythology. These narratives are not merely tales of individual heroism but reflections of the cultural values and ideals of the Norse people. The heroes of Midgard confront overwhelming odds, facing both external monsters and internal struggles with steadfast determination. Their tales remind us that true heroism lies in the courage to face one's fears and the strength to endure adversity.

The legends of Sigurd, Beowulf, and other heroes of Midgard continue to inspire and captivate audiences with their timeless appeal. These stories of dragon slayers and monster hunters resonate with the universal human experience, illustrating the perpetual battle between light and darkness, good and evil. By exploring the epic adventures of these legendary figures, we gain insight into the enduring nature of heroism and the indomitable spirit that defines the human condition.

The Volsungs: A Saga of Fate and Family

The saga of the Volsungs is a rich tapestry of heroism, tragedy, and destiny. This family's lineage is filled with extraordinary figures whose lives are marked by great deeds and profound sorrow. The Volsungs' story is one of the most compelling narratives in Norse mythology, illustrating the relentless pursuit of honor and the inescapable grip of fate.

Sigmund, the legendary patriarch of the Volsung clan, is a figure of immense strength and courage whose life is marked by trials, valor, and the pursuit of honor. His story begins with an act of vengeance and justice, setting the tone for a life of heroic endeavors that would shape the destiny of his lineage.

Sigmund's story unfolds in a time of treachery and betrayal. The Volsung clan, renowned for their bravery and noble heritage, faced a grave injustice at the hands of King Siggeir. Sigmund's sister, Signy, was married to Siggeir, but their union was marred by deceit. Siggeir invited the Volsungs to his hall under the guise of friendship, only to betray them, seeking to destroy the noble family and seize their power.

In the ensuing conflict, Sigmund's father, King Volsung, was killed, and his brothers were captured and brutally slain. Sigmund, however, escaped into the forest with Signy's help, harboring a burning desire for revenge and the restoration of his family's honor. For years, he lived in hiding, gathering his strength and waiting for the opportune moment to strike back at Siggeir.

A pivotal moment in Sigmund's tale occurred at a feast hosted by King Siggeir. Among the guests was a mysterious, one-eyed old man, who was none other than the god Odin in disguise. During the feast, Odin approached the great tree Barnstokkr, which stood in the center of the hall, and plunged a magnificent sword into its trunk. He declared that the sword, which would later be known as Gram, would belong to the one who could pull it free.

Many noble warriors attempted to draw the sword, but all failed. When it was Sigmund's turn, he effortlessly extracted Gram from the tree, signifying his divine favor and destiny for greatness. This act not only marked Sigmund as a hero of legend but also symbolized the restoration of the Volsung honor, as the sword became a powerful symbol of his rightful place as a leader and warrior.

With Gram in his possession, Sigmund embarked on a series of epic adventures. His life was a continuous struggle against formidable foes and supernatural challenges. Alongside his sister Signy, who was deeply loyal to her Volsung blood, Sigmund waged a secret war against Siggeir. Signy, driven by her own desire for vengeance, made great sacrifices, even bearing a son, Sinfjotli, with Sigmund to create a warrior strong enough to aid in their quest for retribution.

The culmination of their vengeance came when Sigmund and Sinfjotli, now grown and trained as a warrior, attacked Siggeir's hall. In a brutal and fiery confrontation, they defeated Siggeir, fulfilling the long-sought vengeance for the Volsung family. This victory, however, was bittersweet, as Signy chose to die alongside her husband, feeling her duty to her family was complete.

After avenging his family, Sigmund continued his heroic journey. He became a king and was known far and wide for his strength and bravery. His reign was marked by battles and conquests, always with Gram at his side. Despite the many challenges he faced, Sigmund's unwavering resolve and formidable strength ensured his continued victories.

His adventures and the tales of his courage were not just personal triumphs but also set the stage for the future glory of the Volsung clan. The heroic exploits of Sigmund would inspire his descendants, especially his son Sigurd, who would go on to become one of the greatest heroes in Norse mythology, slaying the dragon Fafnir and achieving legendary status.

Sigmund's life was not without tragedy. In a fierce battle against the forces of King Lyngvi, Sigmund faced an opponent he could not defeat. As he fought valiantly, Odin appeared again, this time in his true form, and shattered Gram. Without his divine weapon, Sigmund was mortally wounded. As he lay dying, he imparted his legacy to his wife, Hjordis, and their unborn son, Sigurd, entrusting them with the broken pieces of Gram.

Sigmund's death marked the end of his journey but also the beginning of Sigurd's. The broken sword, Gram, would be reforged for Sigurd, who would use it to achieve great deeds, thus continuing the Volsung legacy of heroism and honor.

Sigmund's story is a testament to the enduring themes of Norse mythology: the pursuit of honor, the inevitability of fate, and the heroic struggle against overwhelming odds. His life and deeds not only restored the honor of the Volsung clan but also laid the foundation for the epic sagas that followed, making him a cornerstone of Norse heroic legend.

Sigurd, the greatest of the Volsungs, is a hero whose epic quest and tragic love story are etched in the annals of Norse mythology. His tale is a continuation of the Volsung legacy, filled with heroic deeds, cursed treasures, and the inevitable pull of fate. Guided by his mentor, the cunning dwarf Regin, and armed with the reforged sword Gram, Sigurd embarks on a journey that would cement his place as a legendary hero.

The Slaying of Fafnir

Sigurd's journey begins with the task of slaying the dragon Fafnir, a monstrous creature that guards a hoard of treasure cursed by its original owner, the dwarf Andvari. This treasure, including the powerful ring Andvaranaut, is tainted with a curse that ensures misfortune for all who possess it. Under Regin's tutelage, Sigurd learns of Fafnir's greed and the immense wealth he guards. The treasure's allure and the promise of glory drive Sigurd to take on this perilous challenge.

With Gram in hand, a sword reforged from the shattered blade of his father Sigmund, Sigurd approaches Fafnir's lair. He digs a trench in the path Fafnir takes to drink from a river, and as the dragon slithers over the trench, Sigurd strikes a fatal blow to its heart. As Fafnir lies dying, he warns Sigurd of the curse upon the treasure, a forewarning that Sigurd dismisses, eager to claim his prize.

After the dragon's death, Sigurd tastes Fafnir's blood, gaining the ability to understand the language of birds. This newfound wisdom reveals Regin's treacherous intentions; the birds speak of how Regin plans to betray Sigurd to claim the treasure for himself. Armed with this knowledge, Sigurd preemptively kills Regin, ensuring his safety but also cementing his connection to the cursed gold.

The Tragic Love of Sigurd and Brynhild

One of the most poignant elements of Sigurd's story is his love for Brynhild, a Valkyrie bound by an enchanted sleep. Sigurd, guided by destiny, finds Brynhild encased in a ring of fire and awakens her with a kiss. Their love is immediate and profound, and they pledge themselves to one another. However, the curse of Andvaranaut and the machinations of others soon cast a shadow over their happiness.

Sigurd eventually comes to the court of King Gjuki, where he is given a potion to forget Brynhild and falls in love with Gudrun, the king's daughter. He marries Gudrun, and as a gesture of goodwill, helps her brother, Gunnar, win Brynhild's hand in marriage by using his shape-shifting abilities to take Gunnar's form and pass through the flames surrounding Brynhild.

Brynhild, unaware of the deception, marries Gunnar but soon learns the truth. Her heartbreak and fury are compounded by the realization that

Sigurd, whom she still loves, betrayed her. The curse of the treasure and the manipulations of the court lead to a tragic unraveling. Consumed by despair and seeking revenge, Brynhild plots Sigurd's death, convincing her brother Guttorm to murder him.

In a treacherous act, Guttorm stabs Sigurd while he sleeps, and the hero dies, fulfilling the tragic prophecy tied to the cursed treasure. As he dies, Sigurd laments the loss of Brynhild and the love they shared, a love that was doomed from the start by forces beyond their control. Brynhild, stricken with grief and guilt, takes her own life, requesting to be laid beside Sigurd on the funeral pyre. Their deaths mark a sorrowful end to a tale of love, heroism, and tragic fate.

Sigurd's story is a reflection of the Norse belief in the inevitability of fate and the impermanence of life, no matter how heroic. Despite his unmatched bravery, strength, and the divine favor he seemed to possess, Sigurd could not escape the destiny foretold for him. His life, filled with heroic triumphs and profound love, ultimately succumbed to the inexorable pull of fate and the curse of the treasure.

Sigurd's legacy endures as a testament to the ideals of courage, honor, and the relentless pursuit of glory. His story, intertwined with the complex interplay of fate and free will, illustrates the timeless themes of the Volsung saga. The heroic struggle against overwhelming odds and the tragic consequences of one's actions continue to resonate, making Sigurd a lasting symbol of the Norse heroic ideal.

The Fall of the Volsungs

The saga of the Volsungs is a rich tapestry of loyalty, betrayal, and the relentless force of fate, encapsulating the essence of the Norse heroic ideal. This epic narrative chronicles the triumphs and tragedies of the Volsung family, whose members navigate a world governed by destiny, honor, and vengeance. Throughout their saga, the Volsungs are frequently deceived by those they trust, yet they persist in their quest for justice and glory, demonstrating an unwavering resolve and commitment to their lineage.

The tale begins with Sigmund, the scion of the Volsung clan, who finds himself embroiled in a bitter feud with King Siggeir. This conflict is ignited by a grievous act of betrayal: Siggeir invites the Volsung family to his kingdom under the guise of hospitality, only to ambush them. The Volsung patriarch, King Volsung, is slain, and his sons are captured and brutally executed, save for Sigmund, who escapes with the aid of his sister Signy.

Driven by the need to avenge his family's honor, Sigmund hides in the wilderness, biding his time. The years pass, but Sigmund's thirst for revenge remains unquenched. With the help of Signy, who sacrifices much to aid her brother's cause, Sigmund ultimately exacts his vengeance on Siggeir, destroying him and his household. This victory, however, is tinged with sorrow, as Signy, tormented by the cost of vengeance, chooses to die alongside her husband, despite her complicity in his downfall.

The saga continues with Sigmund's son, Sigurd, whose story intertwines heroism with tragic romance. Sigurd, guided by the dwarf Regin, seeks out and slays the dragon Fafnir, claiming the cursed treasure hoard guarded by the beast. This act solidifies Sigurd's status as a legendary hero, yet the treasure's curse, tied to the ring Andvaranaut, brings nothing but sorrow.

Sigurd's life is further complicated by his love for Brynhild, a Valkyrie whom he awakens from an enchanted sleep. Their love is deep and true, yet doomed from the start. Under the influence of a potion, Sigurd forgets Brynhild and marries another woman, Gudrun, thus setting off a chain of events fueled by misunderstanding and betrayal. Brynhild, deceived into marrying Gudrun's brother Gunnar, feels betrayed by Sigurd's actions and her own fate.

The curse of Andvaranaut and the manipulations of others lead to a tragic climax. Brynhild, consumed by jealousy and sorrow, orchestrates Sigurd's death through her brother Guttorm. As Sigurd dies, he laments the loss of Brynhild and the happiness they might have shared, a poignant reminder of the inevitability of fate and the sorrow it often brings.

The saga's culmination is marked by the fall of the remaining Volsung descendants, each meeting their end with bravery and acceptance of their fates. Gudrun's brothers, including Gunnar and Hogni, face a doomed battle against Atli, Brynhild's vengeful brother. The tragic death of Sigurd and the subsequent downfall of his kin emphasize the harsh reality of fate's inescapable grip.

As the last of the Volsung bloodline faces their end, the saga reflects on the grand design woven by the Norns, the mythological weavers of fate. The Volsung heroes, despite their extraordinary feats and relentless pursuit of honor, cannot escape their predestined outcomes. Their lives and deaths underscore the Norse belief in the inevitability of fate, the transience of life, and the ultimate importance of facing one's destiny with courage and dignity.

Legacy and Reflection

The Volsung saga, with its intricate plot and complex characters, serves as a vivid portrayal of the Norse heroic ideal. It emphasizes the paramount importance of honor and legacy, even in the face of inevitable doom. The Volsungs' tale is a powerful narrative about the profound impact of fate on human lives and the lengths to which individuals will go to uphold their family's honor.

Through the cycles of betrayal and revenge, the Volsungs display an indomitable spirit, continually striving for glory despite knowing their triumphs are fleeting. The saga illustrates the Norse understanding that while fate cannot be changed, the manner in which one meets their destiny defines their honor and legacy.

The story of the Volsungs remains a timeless reminder of the strength and resilience required to navigate the trials of life. It highlights the enduring impact of one's actions on the tapestry of history and the indelible mark left by those who pursue honor and glory, regardless of the odds. Through their saga, the Volsungs continue to inspire with tales of bravery, loyalty, and the relentless pursuit of an honorable legacy, even as they confront the inexorable forces of fate.

Thematic Exploration:

The tales of these heroes explore themes of bravery, fate, and the hero's journey. Their stories are not just about physical strength but also about the inner qualities that define a true hero. The struggle against overwhelming odds, the loyalty to one's kin and comrades, and the acceptance of fate's role in their lives are central to understanding what it means to be a hero in Norse mythology.

Bravery is a core theme in the sagas of the Volsungs and other Norse heroes. Whether it's Sigmund's fierce battles to restore his family's honor or Sigurd's epic quest to slay the dragon Fafnir, these heroes exemplify the courage required to face daunting challenges. Their tales emphasize that true bravery is not just about physical prowess but also about the courage to make difficult decisions, confront one's fears, and endure suffering for a greater cause. This bravery is often portrayed as a noble quality that earns the respect of both gods and men.

Fate, or wyrd, is an inescapable force in Norse mythology. The heroes of the Volsung saga are acutely aware of the role fate plays in their lives. Sigmund's retrieval of the sword Gram, Sigurd's encounter with the cursed treasure, and the tragic love story with Brynhild all highlight how fate interweaves with their actions and decisions. Despite their immense strength and heroic deeds, the Volsungs cannot escape their predestined paths. This acceptance of fate, even when it leads to tragic outcomes, is a defining characteristic of Norse heroes. It underscores the belief that understanding and embracing one's destiny is an integral part of heroism.

The hero's journey is a recurring motif in Norse mythology. The Volsung saga, with its rich narrative of trials, triumphs, and tragedies, perfectly encapsulates this theme. Heroes like Sigmund and Sigurd embark on perilous quests, face formidable foes, and endure personal sacrifices. Their journeys are not only physical but also spiritual, leading to profound transformations. This journey often involves a quest for a significant object, like the cursed treasure, or the fulfillment of a personal mission, such as restoring family honor. Through their trials, these heroes grow, learn, and ultimately become symbols of the ideal Norse warrior.

The tales of the Volsungs and other Norse heroes reflect the values and ideals of the culture from which they originate. Bravery, loyalty, and the acceptance of fate are celebrated as virtues that define true heroism. These themes resonate through the sagas, offering timeless lessons on the nature of courage, the inevitability of destiny, and the transformative power of the hero's journey. Through their stories, we gain insight into the qualities that were revered by the Norse people and the enduring legacy of their heroic traditions.

Call to Action:

As we explored the stories of Sigurd, Beowulf, and the Volsungs, you can now reflect on the qualities that define heroism in your own life. Consider the bravery required to face your challenges, the loyalty to those you hold dear, and the acceptance of the roles we play in the larger tapestry of life. These ancient tales, rich with themes of courage, destiny, and resilience, serve as timeless reminders of the inner strength we all possess.

Think about the dragons you must slay in your own journey, whether they are external obstacles or internal struggles. Like Sigurd, who faced the fearsome Fafnir, summon the courage to confront your fears head-on. Recognize the importance of loyalty and honor in your relationships, just as Beowulf remained steadfast in his duty to protect his people. Embrace the acceptance of fate, understanding that some aspects of life are beyond our control, yet we can still navigate them with dignity and strength.

Let these stories inspire you to embrace your inner hero. Draw strength from the legacy of these legendary figures and their unyielding spirit. As you navigate the challenges and triumphs of your own life, remember the lessons of Norse mythology: bravery, loyalty, and the acceptance of destiny. By embodying these virtues, you can face your personal battles with the same valor and resilience that defined the heroes of old.

May the tales of Sigurd, Beowulf, and the Volsungs ignite a spark within you, encouraging you to rise to the occasion and fulfill your own heroic potential. Let these myths guide you as you confront the dragons in your journey, and may you find inspiration in their timeless wisdom. Embrace your inner hero and make your mark on the tapestry of life.

I Would Love Your Review!

Thank you for embarking on this exciting journey into Viking lore with *Norse Mythology, Legends and Legacy*! This book was written to help you explore the fascinating myths of Odin, Thor, Loki, and other legendary figures through engaging storytelling paired with modern insights.

If you enjoyed diving into the world of Norse gods and legends, we would truly appreciate hearing your thoughts! Your review will help other readers discover the captivating stories of Viking culture and mythology.

What Should You Include in Your Review?

What did you find most interesting about the myths of Odin, Thor, or Loki?

Was the storytelling engaging and easy to follow?

Did you learn something new about Norse mythology that surprised you?

How did you feel about the way ancient legends were connected to modern ideas?

Your feedback means the world to me, and it helps more readers find and enjoy this journey through Viking myths.

Your feedback means the world to me, and it helps more readers find and enjoy this journey through Viking myths.

How to Leave Your Review

Scan this QR code

OR

https://www.amazon.com/review/create-
review/?ie=UTF8&channel=glance-detail&asin=B0DGR9DNSX

Share your thoughts with other readers. You can be brief or detailed—whatever you feel comfortable with!

Thank you for your support, and we hope *Norse Mythology, Legends and Legacy* has inspired you with the powerful stories of Viking lore!

Best regards,

Shari Claire

Chapter 4:

Norse Mythology and Viking

Culture

Norse mythology is not just a collection of stories but a reflection of the values, fears, and aspirations of the Viking culture. These myths provided a framework for understanding the world, guiding everything from personal conduct to societal norms.

The Foundation of Viking Beliefs

Norse mythology formed the bedrock of Viking beliefs, infusing their world with a sense of divine order and cosmic significance. The Vikings believed that their actions were closely observed by the gods, and living a life of honor and bravery was crucial for gaining their favor.

The cosmology of Norse mythology, with its nine interconnected worlds held together by the great ash tree Yggdrasil, provided a structured universe where every action had meaning and consequence. This interconnectedness reinforced the belief that the gods were actively involved in the affairs of humans, guiding and judging their actions. The gods, such as Odin, Thor, and Freyja, were not distant deities but powerful beings who could be called upon for aid, protection, and wisdom.

The myths were more than just stories; they were moral and ethical guides that informed the Vikings' sense of duty, courage, and justice. The concept of wyrd, or fate, was central to their worldview, suggesting that while certain aspects of life were predestined, individuals still had the responsibility to face their destiny with honor. This belief in fate and the gods' oversight encouraged a strong warrior ethos and a culture where bravery in battle was the highest virtue.

Moreover, rituals and sacrifices were integral to maintaining the favor of the gods. The Vikings engaged in blóts, where animals, and sometimes humans, were sacrificed to appease the gods and secure their blessings. These ceremonies, often conducted by chieftains or priests known as gothi, were crucial for ensuring the community's well-being and success in endeavors such as farming, trading, and warfare.

Norse mythology also emphasized the importance of legacy and reputation. The stories of heroes like Sigmund, Sigurd, and Beowulf were recounted to inspire and instruct, showing that one's deeds could achieve immortality through tales and songs. The pursuit of honor, even in the face of insurmountable odds, was a way to ensure that one's name would be remembered and celebrated long after death.

In summary, Norse mythology was the foundation upon which Viking society was built. It provided a framework for understanding the world and one's place in it, emphasizing the importance of honor, bravery, and the pursuit of a noble legacy. Through their actions and rituals, the Vikings sought to align themselves with the divine order and gain the favor of the gods, ensuring their place in the cosmic balance.

The Concept of Fate

Central to Norse belief was the concept of fate, or wyrd. The Norns, three mythical beings named Urd (Past), Verdandi (Present), and Skuld (Future), were believed to spin the threads of fate for all beings, from gods to mortals. These three beings resided at the base of Yggdrasil, the World Tree, weaving the destinies of all creatures into an intricate tapestry that formed the fabric of existence.

The Norns' control over fate underscored the inevitability of destiny in Norse mythology. Every event, from the grand schemes of the gods to the everyday actions of humans, was believed to be part of a predetermined path. This belief in a fixed destiny did not negate the importance of individual action, however. Instead, it emphasized the need to confront one's fate with bravery and honor. The Norse admired those who faced their predetermined ends with stoic courage and resilience, seeing these qualities as the true measure of a hero.

For the Vikings, fate was an ever-present force that could not be escaped, only embraced. This acceptance of wyrd cultivated a culture that valued courage and honor above all. Heroes like Sigurd and Beowulf were revered not just for their physical prowess but for their willingness to face their destinies head-on, regardless of the outcome. The inevitability of fate reinforced the idea that how one lived and faced challenges was of paramount importance.

The belief in fate also shaped the Vikings' view of the afterlife. The idea that warriors who died bravely in battle would be taken to Valhalla, Odin's hall, or Fólkvangr, Freyja's field, where they would be honored and live eternally, was deeply rooted in the concept of wyrd. This belief provided a powerful incentive for living a life of valor and honor, as it assured a noble and glorious end.

In summary, the concept of fate, or wyrd, was central to Norse belief, influencing every aspect of Viking life. The Norns' weaving of destiny highlighted the inevitability of fate and the importance of meeting one's end with courage and dignity. This belief system instilled a profound sense of purpose and honor in the Vikings, guiding their actions and reinforcing their cultural values.

The Afterlife

The Vikings held complex views on the afterlife, shaped profoundly by their rich mythology. These beliefs provided both comfort and motivation, particularly for warriors who valued honor and bravery above all else. The afterlife destinations varied based on the nature of one's death and their deeds in life, reflecting the values and societal norms of Viking culture.

Valhalla: The Hall of the Slain

Warriors who died bravely in battle were believed in Norse mythology to be taken by the Valkyries, the warrior maidens serving Odin, the All-Father and chief of the Aesir gods. The Valkyries, whose name means "Choosers of the Slain," were depicted as majestic and formidable figures, often riding winged horses or wolves across the skies, adorned in shining armor and carrying spears. They would descend upon the battlefields, weaving through the chaos of war to select the most valiant of the fallen warriors. These chosen heroes were then escorted to Valhalla, the great hall of the slain located in Asgard, the celestial realm of the gods.

Valhalla was depicted as a majestic and grand hall with a roof made of golden shields and spears, its walls adorned with gleaming armor, and its rafters fashioned from massive spears. It was so vast that it could accommodate all the warriors chosen throughout time. The hall had 540 doors, each wide enough for 800 warriors to march through side by side, allowing the Einherjar to exit when the time came to fight in Ragnarok swiftly, the prophesied end of the world. The ceiling was thatched with golden shields, and the hall was illuminated by the glow of countless swords, adding to its otherworldly splendor.

The fallen warriors, known as Einherjar, would reside in Valhalla under Odin's watchful eye. These warriors were considered the bravest and most skilled, having proven their worth through their heroic deaths. Each day in Valhalla, the Einherjar would don their armor and engage in glorious battle against one another on the plains surrounding the hall. They fought with full vigor and ferocity, honing their combat skills and testing their mettle. Despite the intensity of these battles, any wounds or deaths sustained were miraculously healed by evening, ensuring that the warriors were restored to full health for the nightly festivities.

In the evenings, the Einherjar would gather in Valhalla for grand feasts that were the epitome of indulgence and camaraderie. They were served by the Valkyries, who attended to them with mead drawn from the udder of the goat Heiðrún, which provided an endless supply of the finest mead. The meat came from the boar Sæhrímnir, which was slaughtered and cooked each night by the cook Andhrímnir in the cauldron Eldhrímnir. Remarkably, Sæhrímnir would be resurrected each morning, ready to be prepared again, symbolizing the eternal abundance of Valhalla.

During these feasts, the warriors would recount tales of their past exploits, share wisdom, and celebrate their heroic deeds. The atmosphere was one of perpetual joy and honor, strengthening the bonds between the warriors and reinforcing their commitment to their cause. The merriment also served to bolster their spirits for the days of training and battle that lay ahead.

This cycle of daily battles and nightly feasts was not merely for enjoyment but served a critical purpose. The Einherjar were being meticulously prepared for Ragnarok, the ultimate battle between the gods and the forces of chaos, led by Loki and his monstrous offspring, including the Midgard Serpent and the Fenrir Wolf. During Ragnarok, these warriors would fight alongside Odin and the Aesir gods against giants, fire demons, and other malevolent beings in an epic struggle that would determine the fate of the cosmos. The training and honing of their skills in Valhalla were essential to ensure they were ready to face this cataclysmic event.

The promise of Valhalla was a powerful incentive for Vikings to display courage and valor in battle. The belief that a glorious death could lead to an eternal life of honor among the gods encouraged warriors to face even the most daunting battles without fear. This aspiration was deeply ingrained in Viking culture, where dying in combat was considered the most honorable end a warrior could achieve. It ensured that their legacy would live on through their bravery, and their names would be immortalized in sagas and songs passed down through generations.

Valhalla also held significant cultural importance beyond the individual warrior. It reinforced societal values such as honor, bravery, loyalty, and the warrior ethos that were central to Viking society. The concept of an afterlife where the bravest warriors continued to fight and feast resonated deeply within their communities, shaping their attitudes toward life and death. It provided a framework where the hardships and dangers of their lives, whether in battle or during voyages across treacherous seas, were given meaning and purpose within the grand tapestry of their mythology.

Moreover, the Valkyries themselves were fascinating figures within Norse mythology. They were not only escorts to Valhalla but also served mead to the Einherjar and could influence the outcomes of battles according to Odin's will. Some sagas suggest that Valkyries could even become lovers of mortal heroes, further intertwining the mortal and divine realms. Their presence emphasized the importance of fate and destiny, as they were agents who enacted Odin's choices regarding who would live and who would die in battle.

Additionally, the imagery of Valhalla and the Valkyries influenced art, poetry, and storytelling within Norse culture. Skaldic poets often composed intricate verses that celebrated great warriors' deeds and Valhalla's glory. These tales served to inspire future generations to uphold these ideals, reinforcing the cultural identity and values of the Viking people.

The concept of Valhalla also highlighted the close relationship between the mortal world and the divine in Norse belief. The idea that a mortal could ascend to live among the gods was both empowering and motivating. It suggested that through one's actions and choices, particularly acts of bravery and honor, an individual could transcend the ordinary and achieve something extraordinary.

In conclusion, the belief in Valhalla and the role of the Valkyries served as profound motivators for warriors in Viking society. It encapsulated the ultimate honor and reward for those who lived and died by the sword, ensuring their valor was recognized and immortalized. The promise of an afterlife filled with eternal glory, camaraderie, and purpose reinforced the societal emphasis on martial prowess and the virtues of bravery and honor. This belief system shaped the ethos of the Viking Age and left a lasting legacy in the annals of Norse mythology, influencing not only their own culture but also captivating people's imagination throughout the centuries that followed.

Fólkvangr: Freyja's Realm

Another desirable afterlife destination in Norse mythology was Fólkvangr, which translates to "Field of the People" or "Field of the Host," ruled by the goddess Freyja. Freyja was one of the most prominent and revered deities in the Norse pantheon, associated with love, beauty, fertility, war, and magic. She was a member of the Vanir, a group of gods associated with nature and fertility, who resided alongside the Æsir gods like Odin and Thor after the two groups reconciled their differences. Freyja's multifaceted nature made her an essential figure in Norse beliefs, embodying both the nurturing and fierce aspects of existence.

In the myths, it is said that Freyja claimed half of the warriors slain in battle, sharing the honor with Odin, who took the other half to Valhalla. This arrangement is mentioned in the poem *Grímnismál* from the Poetic

Edda, where Odin states: *"Fólkvangr is the ninth; there, Freyja directs the seating in the hall. Half the slain she chooses every day, and half Odin owns."*

Fólkvangr was envisioned as a vast, lush meadow or field where the chosen warriors would reside after death. Unlike Valhalla, where warriors prepared endlessly for the events of Ragnarök by engaging in daily battles, Fólkvangr was seen as a more peaceful and harmonious realm. Here, the warriors could rest, enjoy feasts, and partake in the pleasures of Freyja's hall, Sessrúmnir, which means "Seat Room" or "Hall of Many Seats." This hall was not just spacious, but also welcoming, reflecting Freyja's generous and hospitable nature.

Freyja's role in selecting the slain warriors highlighted her sovereignty and significance in the Norse cosmology. As a goddess who presided over both love and war, her claim over the fallen heroes underscored the duality of life and death, love and battle. She was known to ride a chariot pulled by two cats or to fly over battlefields in the form of a falcon, searching for those worthy of joining her in Fólkvangr. This portrayal emphasized her active involvement in the affairs of both gods and humans.

The dual honor of being chosen by either Odin or Freyja underscored the high value placed on martial prowess and heroism in Viking society. Warriors aspired to die bravely in battle, believing that such a death would grant them a place in either Valhalla or Fólkvangr. This belief reinforced the cultural ideals of courage, honor, and the warrior ethos that were central to Norse society. It also reflected the understanding that valor could be rewarded in different ways, offering a choice between the eternal battles of Valhalla and the peaceful rewards of Fólkvangr.

Freyja's association with love, beauty, and fertility added layers of meaning to the afterlife in Fólkvangr. It wasn't just a place of rest but also one of joy, abundance, and perhaps even romantic fulfillment. The warriors in her realm could experience the pleasures of life that they may have sacrificed during their mortal existence. This aspect made Fólkvangr an appealing destination for those who sought a more serene afterlife.

Moreover, Freyja was a master of seiðr, a form of Norse magic concerned with fate and prophecy. She was said to have taught this art to Odin, further illustrating her powerful and influential role among the gods. Her mastery of magic and connections to the mystical realms added to the allure of Fólkvangr as a place where one could continue to explore the mysteries of existence under the guidance of a wise and potent goddess.

The existence of multiple afterlife destinations like Valhalla and Fólkvangr reflects the Norse people's complex views on death and the afterlife. It wasn't a monolithic concept but rather a multifaceted one, where the soul's destination could vary based on how one lived and died. This diversity acknowledged the different paths a person could take and the various deities who might claim them.

Fólkvangr's portrayal as a peaceful and prosperous realm also speaks to the Norse appreciation for balance. While they glorified battle and valor, they also recognized the value of peace, rest, and the more nurturing aspects of life, embodied by Freyja. This balance is evident in their mythology and rituals, which celebrated both the warrior's strength and the farmer's toil, the harshness of winter and the fertility of spring.

In addition, Freyja's claim over half of the slain warriors symbolizes the equal importance of female divine figures in Norse mythology. It highlights the respect and reverence for goddesses who wielded significant power and influence. Freyja was not just a passive figure but an active participant in the cosmos's workings, guiding souls, influencing fate, and embodying essential aspects of life.

In summary, Fólkvangr represented more than just an afterlife destination; it was a manifestation of Freyja's complex character and the values of Viking society. The warriors chosen by Freyja were honored for their bravery and embraced into a realm that celebrated peace, prosperity, and the joys of existence. The shared honor between Odin and Freyja in claiming the fallen highlighted the importance of both deities and reinforced the cultural ideals surrounding warfare, heroism, and the afterlife. This duality underscored a society that valued both the fierce and the gentle, the warrior and the nurturer, reflecting a nuanced understanding of the human experience.

Hel: The Realm of the Dead

For those who did not die in battle, the afterlife destination was often Hel, a realm ruled by the goddess Hel, one of Loki's children. Contrary to some later interpretations, Hel was not a place of punishment but rather a neutral, shadowy realm where those who died of illness, old age, or other non-violent means would reside. It was a place of rest and reflection, where the dead would exist in a state of neither bliss nor torment. Hel's domain was essential in the Viking understanding of the afterlife, offering a place for those who led honorable lives but did not die in combat.

The Vikings believed that proper rituals and burial practices were crucial for ensuring a favorable afterlife. Funeral rites often involved elaborate ceremonies, including ship burials for the nobility, where the deceased were laid to rest with their belongings, weapons, and sometimes even sacrificed animals or slaves, to accompany them into the afterlife. These practices reflected the belief that the dead needed these items to maintain their status and comfort in the next world.

The use of rune stones and memorial markers was also common, serving both to honor the deceased and to provide a tangible link between the living and the dead. These stones often included inscriptions that recounted the deeds and lineage of the deceased, ensuring that their memory would endure.

The Viking views on the afterlife were more than just religious beliefs; they were integral to the social and moral fabric of Viking culture. The promise of Valhalla or Fólkvangr motivated warriors to seek glory in battle, while the acceptance of Hel provided a dignified end for those who lived honorable lives outside of combat. These beliefs reinforced the values of courage, honor, and loyalty, which were central to Viking society.

In summary, the Vikings' views on the afterlife were deeply intertwined with their mythology and cultural values. The destinations of Valhalla, Fólkvangr, and Hel reflected the importance of bravery, honor, and proper conduct in life and death. These beliefs not only guided the actions of the living but also ensured that the legacy of the dead would be remembered and revered.

The Ausa Vatni Ceremony

One of the most important rituals for a newborn was the ausa vatni, or "sprinkling with water," ceremony. This ritual marked the child's acceptance into the community and was often conducted by the father or another significant family member. During the ceremony, the baby was sprinkled with water, symbolizing purification and a fresh start. This act was not a baptism in the Christian sense but a traditional Norse ritual that affirmed the child's place in the world and their right to protection and care within the community.

The ausa vatni ceremony was also when the child received their name. Naming a child was a serious and meaningful event, as names were believed to carry power and significance. Parents often chose names of ancestors or gods, hoping to invoke the qualities and protection associated with those names. For example, a child named Thorolf might be expected to inherit the strength and courage of the god Thor, while a girl named Freydis might be seen as embodying the beauty and fertility associated with the goddess Freyja.

Naming After Ancestors

Naming a child after an ancestor was a common practice that reinforced family ties and honored the memory of those who had passed. It was believed that by giving a child the name of a respected ancestor, the qualities and virtues of that ancestor would be passed on to the child. This practice helped to keep the memory of the ancestors alive within the family and ensured that their legacy continued through the generations.

The name given to a child also served as a link to the family's history and stories. It was a way of preserving the lineage and the deeds of those who came before, embedding the child in a web of relationships and expectations. This tradition of naming after ancestors underscored the importance of family heritage and continuity in Viking culture.

Invoking the Gods

In addition to naming children after ancestors, parents might also choose names that invoked the gods, seeking their favor and protection for the newborn. Names like Thorstein ("Thor's stone") or Astrid ("God's strength") were common, reflecting the deep connection the Vikings felt with their deities. By invoking the gods through their children's names, Viking parents expressed their desire for divine support in their child's life journey.

The belief in the protective power of names extended beyond just the naming ceremony. Throughout their lives, individuals would carry the attributes and blessings of the names they bore, serving as a constant reminder of their connection to the divine and their cultural heritage.

Community and Acceptance

The ausa vatni ceremony and the act of naming were also crucial for integrating the newborn into the community. These rituals signified the child's acceptance and the community's commitment to their well-being. In a society where kinship and communal bonds were vital for survival, these rituals ensured that every new member was recognized and valued.

The ceremony often involved a gathering of family and community members, who would witness the ritual and celebrate the new addition to their society. This communal aspect of the ceremony reinforced social bonds and emphasized the collective responsibility of raising and protecting the child.

In summary, birth and naming rituals in Viking culture were profound expressions of family heritage, divine connection, and communal responsibility. The ausa vatni ceremony, which translates to "sprinkling with water," was a pivotal ritual performed shortly after a child's birth. The newborn was sprinkled with water during this ceremony, symbolizing purification, acceptance, and the child's formal introduction into the family and community. This act was not merely a private family matter but a significant communal event, often attended by extended family members and neighbors who would bear witness to the child's entry into society.

Naming children after esteemed ancestors or revered gods and goddesses was another essential aspect of Viking birth rituals. By bestowing a name that held historical or divine significance, families sought to honor their lineage and forge a spiritual connection between the child and the powerful figures of their past. This tradition was believed to confer the virtues, strengths, and protections associated with those namesakes onto the child. For instance, a child named after Thor might be hoped to inherit qualities of strength and bravery, while one named after a respected grandparent would carry forward the family's legacy and honor.

These rituals were essential in embedding the newborn into the very fabric of Viking society. The ausa vatni ceremony and the meaningful naming practices ensured that the child was not only recognized by the community but also connected to the ancestral and divine forces that shaped their world. The communal involvement in these ceremonies underscored a shared responsibility for the upbringing and welfare of the child, reflecting the tightly knit nature of Viking communities where each member played a role in the collective well-being.

Moreover, these practices served to reinforce social bonds and cultural continuity. By linking the new generation to the past through names and rituals, the Vikings maintained a strong sense of identity and cohesion within their society. It was a way of passing down traditions, values, and stories that defined who they were as a people. The child, carrying the legacy and protection of their forebears and deities, was seen as the living embodiment of the community's past, present, and future.

As the child embarked on their life's journey, these early rituals provided a foundation of belonging and purpose. They were constantly reminded of their heritage and the expectations that came with it, fostering a sense of duty and pride. The divine connection implied by their name and the blessings received during the ausa vatni ceremony were thought to offer guidance and protection throughout their lives, influencing their actions and decisions in alignment with the values of their society.

In essence, Viking birth and naming rituals were multifaceted ceremonies rich with symbolism and significance. They celebrated new life while honoring the ancestral and divine forces central to Viking belief systems. These practices ensured that each individual was deeply rooted in their heritage, spiritually connected to the gods, and embraced by their

92

community. By doing so, they perpetuated the cultural values, traditions, and social structures that were fundamental to the Viking way of life, ensuring the continuity and resilience of their society across generations.

Seasonal Festivals

The Vikings celebrated numerous festivals throughout the year that aligned with agricultural cycles and significant mythological events. These festivals were not only times of communal celebration and feasting but also played a crucial role in reinforcing social bonds and ensuring the gods' favor for the coming year. Among these, the most significant was Yule, a midwinter festival that honored the rebirth of the sun and the god Balder.

Yule: The Midwinter Festival

Yule, or Jól, was the most important festival in the Viking calendar, celebrated around the time of the winter solstice. This festival marked the rebirth of the sun after the longest night of the year, symbolizing the return of light and the promise of renewed life and growth. Yule was a time of great celebration, featuring feasts, sacrifices, and various rituals designed to honor the gods and ensure their blessings for the year ahead.

One of the key deities honored during Yule was Balder, the god of light and purity, whose death and prophesied return were central to Norse mythology. The story of Balder's death at the hands of Loki and the subsequent mourning by the gods underscored themes of loss and renewal, which were particularly poignant during the dark days of winter. By celebrating Balder's connection to the sun and light, the Vikings expressed their hope for the sun's return and the end of winter's hardships.

Feasts and Sacrifices

Feasting was a central element of Yule and other Viking festivals. These communal meals were lavish affairs, featuring abundant food and drink. The feasts were not merely about sustenance but were symbolic acts of communal solidarity and thanksgiving. Sharing food and drink reinforced social bonds within the community and between families, fostering a sense of unity and mutual support.

Sacrifices, or blóts, were another critical component of Viking festivals. These could include animal sacrifices, offerings of food and drink, and sometimes even human sacrifices, though the latter were rare. The purpose of these sacrifices was to honor the gods and ancestors, seeking their favor and protection. The blood of the sacrificed animals was often sprinkled on the altars, idols, and participants, believed to carry the divine blessing.

During Yule, sacrifices were made to ensure a bountiful harvest in the coming year, the health and prosperity of the community, and the favor of the gods. These rituals reflected the deep connection the Vikings felt with their deities and the natural cycles that governed their lives.

Communal Gatherings and Rituals

95

In addition to feasts and sacrifices, Yule and other festivals were times for various communal activities and rituals. These gatherings included storytelling, singing, dancing, and games, all of which played a role in reinforcing cultural traditions and communal ties. The long winter nights provided an opportunity for the community to come together, share stories of their ancestors and gods, and celebrate their shared heritage.

One of the enduring traditions from Yule is the burning of the Yule log, a large log that was kept burning throughout the festival. This practice symbolized warmth, light, and the continuity of life, and its ashes were often kept for good luck throughout the year.

Other Seasonal Festivals

Beyond Yule, the Vikings celebrated several other significant festivals throughout the year, each aligned with key agricultural and mythological events.

Dísablót: Held in late winter or early spring, this festival was dedicated to the dísir, female spirits or deities associated with fertility and protection. It was a time to honor the ancestors and seek blessings for the coming planting season.

Ostara: Celebrated around the spring equinox, Ostara was a festival of renewal and fertility, associated with the goddess Eostre. This festival marked the beginning of the agricultural year, with rituals to ensure a successful planting season.

Midsummer: The summer solstice, or Midsummer, was a celebration of the sun at its highest point. It was a time of joy and abundance, with feasting, dancing, and rituals to honor the gods and ensure continued prosperity.

Winter Nights: Celebrated in late autumn, Winter Nights marked the end of the harvest and the beginning of winter. It was a time to honor the

96

spirits and ancestors, with sacrifices and feasts to thank them for the harvest and seek their protection during the harsh winter months.

Cultural Impact

These seasonal festivals were integral to Viking life, providing a rhythm to the year and a sense of continuity and community. They reflected the Vikings' deep connection to the natural world and their reliance on the cycles of nature for survival. The festivals also reinforced the social and religious structures of Viking society, ensuring that each member of the community understood their place within the larger cosmological and social order.

In summary, the seasonal festivals of the Vikings were rich with cultural and religious significance, providing a means to honor the gods, celebrate communal bonds, and ensure the favor of the divine forces that governed their world. These celebrations, particularly Yule, were central to the Vikings' way of life, reflecting their values, beliefs, and the cyclical nature of existence.

Marriage and Family

Marriage was a cornerstone of Viking society, serving as a personal union and a strategic alliance between families and clans. The institution of marriage was crucial for maintaining social order, ensuring the continuity of lineage, and strengthening political and economic bonds. Viking wedding ceremonies were elaborate affairs steeped in ritual and symbolism, reflecting the importance of family ties and the merging of kinship networks.

Arranged Marriages and Alliances

In Viking society, families often arranged marriages to solidify alliances, expand influence, and secure economic stability. These unions were negotiated with careful consideration of the social and political advantages they could bring. Marriages were seen as strategic tools to forge alliances between powerful families and clans, thus playing a significant role in the broader tapestry of Viking politics and society.

The arrangement process involved negotiations between the bride and groom's families, focusing on dowries and bride prices. The dowry, provided by the bride's family, included land, livestock, and household goods, which would contribute to the new household's wealth. The bride price, paid by the groom's family, was a form of compensation for the bride's family, acknowledging the transfer of their daughter to another household.

Wedding Ceremonies

Viking wedding ceremonies were elaborate and imbued with ritual significance. These ceremonies typically took place over several days and involved various customs designed to symbolize the union of two families and the continuity of lineage.

One of the key rituals was the exchange of swords. The groom would present his ancestral sword to the bride, symbolizing the transfer of protection and the bride's entry into his family. In return, the bride would give a dowry sword, signifying her family's support and the merging of their lineage with the groom's. This exchange underscored the martial and protective responsibilities that came with marriage.

The exchange of rings was another significant ritual, symbolizing the binding contract between the couple and their families. These rings were often placed on the hilt of the swords exchanged, further emphasizing the intertwined destinies of the bride and groom.

The wedding feast was a central element of the celebration, where family and friends gathered to honor the couple and their union. This communal meal, often featuring abundant food and drink, reinforced social bonds and celebrated the joining of two families. Toasts to the gods, ancestors, and the couple's future were made, invoking blessings and favor for the newlyweds.

Family Ties and Kinship

In Viking culture, family ties and kinship were paramount. The sagas, or epic stories of the Norse people, often highlight themes of loyalty, honor, and the duties owed to one's family. The family, or clan, was the primary social unit, providing support, protection, and identity to its members.

Loyalty to one's family was considered a sacred duty, and individuals were expected to prioritize their family's honor and interests above their own. This loyalty extended to avenging wrongs against family members, maintaining the family's reputation, and ensuring the welfare of future generations. The strong emphasis on kinship is evident in the sagas, where characters frequently act out of a sense of duty to their family and lineage.

The role of family also extended to the upbringing and education of children. Children were taught the values and traditions of their family from a young age, with a strong focus on the skills and knowledge necessary for survival and success in Viking society. This included martial training, agricultural skills, and an understanding of the legal and social customs of their community.

The Role of Women in Marriage and Family

Women played a vital role in Viking marriages and family life. While marriages were often arranged, women had a degree of agency, especially in their daily lives and household management. Viking women were responsible for running the household, managing servants, and ensuring the smooth operation of the family's economic activities.

Women could also inherit property and wield significant influence within their families. They were often involved in the negotiation of marriages and the management of family estates. In some cases, women acted as heads of households in the absence or death of their husbands, showcasing their importance in maintaining family continuity and stability.

Cultural Impact

The institution of marriage and the importance of family in Viking society were deeply intertwined with their cultural values and social structure. Marriage ceremonies and family ties reflected the Vikings' emphasis on loyalty, honor, and the continuity of lineage. These elements were crucial for the maintenance of social order and the stability of Viking communities.

The sagas' portrayal of family dynamics and the rituals surrounding marriage provide valuable insights into the social fabric of Viking society. They highlight the interconnectedness of individuals within their kinship networks and the collective responsibilities that bound them together.

In summary, marriage and family were vital institutions in Viking society, serving both personal and strategic purposes. Wedding ceremonies, with their rich rituals and symbolism, marked the union of families and the continuity of lineage. Family ties and kinship were central to the Vikings' identity, shaping their actions and ensuring the stability and prosperity of their communities. These values and traditions, preserved in the sagas, continue to offer a window into the complexities of Viking life and culture.

Funeral Rites

Funeral customs in Viking society were elaborate and deeply symbolic, reflecting their beliefs about the afterlife and the importance of honoring the deceased. These rites were designed to ensure a safe passage to the afterlife and to celebrate the life and status of the individual. The grandeur of the funeral often correlated with the deceased's social status, with high-status individuals receiving particularly elaborate send-offs.

Grave Goods

One of the most distinctive aspects of Viking funeral rites was the inclusion of grave goods. These items were believed to be necessary for the deceased's journey to the afterlife and their existence there. The nature and quantity of these goods varied depending on the deceased's status and wealth

102

but commonly included weapons, jewelry, clothing, tools, and household items.

For warriors, weapons such as swords, axes, and shields were included, signifying their role and honor as fighters. These items were not only practical for the afterlife but also served as symbols of the deceased's earthly achievements and status. Jewelry and fine clothing were also common, reflecting the individual's wealth and social standing. Everyday items like combs, cooking utensils, and tools indicated a continuation of daily life in the afterlife, emphasizing the belief that the next world mirrored the present one.

Ship Burials

Among the most remarkable Viking funerals were ship burials, reserved for chieftains, nobles, and other high-status individuals. The ship, a symbol of journey and exploration, was used to represent the deceased's voyage to the otherworld. These burials were grand events, involving significant community participation and elaborate rituals.

In a ship burial, the deceased's body was placed on a boat or a stone ship, along with their grave goods. The ship was then either buried or set adrift. Sometimes, a large burial mound was constructed over the ship, creating an impressive monument to the deceased. The ship symbolized the journey to the afterlife, while the grave goods ensured the deceased was well-equipped for the next world.

The most famous ship burials include the Oseberg Ship and the Gokstad Ship in Norway, which contained richly adorned ships with a wealth of grave goods, indicating the high status of the individuals buried there. These archaeological finds provide invaluable insights into Viking funeral practices and the importance of the ship as a funerary symbol.

Cremation and Burial

While ship burials were reserved for the elite, cremation was a common practice among the broader Viking population. Cremation was believed to release the soul from the body, allowing it to travel to the afterlife. The ashes of the deceased were often buried in urns or scattered in specific locations, sometimes accompanied by a stone marker or cairn.

Burial mounds, or tumuli, were another significant feature of Viking funerary practices. These mounds were constructed over the graves of important individuals and served as lasting monuments to their lives and achievements. The size and complexity of these mounds varied, with larger mounds indicating higher status.

Funerary pyres were also a part of the cremation process, involving large fires where the body and grave goods were burned together. This practice was often accompanied by rituals and offerings to the gods, seeking their favor and ensuring the deceased's safe passage to the afterlife.

Rituals and Ceremonies

Funeral rites were rich with rituals and ceremonies that reflected the community's respect for the deceased and their beliefs about the afterlife. These ceremonies included sacrifices, offerings, and various forms of commemorations.

Sacrifices, or blóts, were performed to honor the gods and seek their protection for the deceased. These could include animal sacrifices, offerings of food and drink. These rituals were meant to appease the gods and ensure that the deceased was welcomed into the afterlife.

Eulogies and songs, known as drápur, were often composed and performed to commemorate the deceased's life and achievements. These poetic tributes highlighted the individual's virtues, heroic deeds, and contributions to their community, ensuring their memory would live on.

The community played a significant role in the funeral process, with family, friends, and fellow villagers participating in the rituals and ceremonies. This collective involvement underscored the social cohesion and shared values of the Viking society, as well as the importance of honoring and remembering the dead.

Symbolism of Funeral Rites

The elaborate nature of Viking funeral rites reflected their profound respect for the dead and their belief in an afterlife. The rituals and grave goods symbolized the transition from the physical world to the spiritual realm, ensuring that the deceased was well-prepared for their journey.

The use of ships in funerals, whether through burial or cremation, highlighted the significance of travel and exploration in Viking culture. Ships were not only practical vehicles but also powerful symbols of transition and the journey between worlds. This symbolism extended to the idea of the afterlife itself, viewed as a continuation of the earthly life, where the dead would require their possessions and skills.

In summary, Viking funeral rites were intricate and symbolic ceremonies that honored the deceased and ensured their safe passage to the afterlife. From the inclusion of grave goods to the grand ship burials of the elite, these practices reflected the Vikings' beliefs about death and the afterlife, their respect for lineage and legacy, and the importance of community in commemorating and supporting the transition of the dead.

Warfare and Honor

Warfare was a central aspect of Viking life, and their mythology glorified the warrior ethos. The Vikings were renowned for their martial prowess, fearlessness in battle, and the cultural importance placed on honor and bravery. The concept of *drengskapr*, or warrior honor, was deeply embedded in their culture, influencing their actions on and off the battlefield.

The Warrior Ethos

The Vikings celebrated the warrior ethos, a set of values emphasizing courage, strength, and loyalty. Their mythology reflected this ethos, where gods and heroes were often depicted as mighty warriors who achieved great deeds through their martial abilities. The tales of gods like Thor and heroes like Sigurd exemplified the virtues of bravery, honor, and the relentless pursuit of glory.

For the Vikings, dying in battle was considered the highest honor. Those who fell in combat were believed to be chosen by the Valkyries to join Odin in Valhalla, the hall of the slain. In Valhalla, these warriors would prepare for the final battle of Ragnarok, continuing to fight and feast in preparation for the end times. This belief in an honorable afterlife for fallen warriors underscored the importance of courage and the acceptance of death as a natural and honorable part of life.

The Concept of Drengskapr

Drengskapr was a core value in Viking society, encompassing the qualities of bravery, honor, loyalty, and generosity. A *drengr*, or honorable warrior, was expected to exhibit these traits in all aspects of life. This concept extended beyond the battlefield to everyday interactions and personal conduct.

A true *drengr* was loyal to their lord and comrades, showing unwavering support and readiness to fight alongside them. Betrayal or cowardice was considered the gravest dishonor, and those who displayed such traits were shunned and disgraced. Generosity was also a key component of *drengskapr*, with warriors expected to share their wealth and success with their companions and community.

The sagas of the Norse people are rich with tales of drengskapr. These stories, passed down through generations, highlight the virtues and flaws of legendary heroes, offering insights into the values of the Viking Age.

Egil Skallagrimsson

Egil Skallagrimsson is one of the most iconic figures in Norse literature, known for his exceptional prowess as both a warrior and a poet. His story is told in *Egil's Saga*, which portrays him as a complex character with a fierce temper and a deep sense of loyalty to his family and friends. Despite his rough exterior, Egil embodies drengskapr through his unwavering commitment to those he cares about and his adherence to the codes of honor.

One of the most famous examples of Egil's drengskapr is his confrontation with King Eirik Bloodaxe. After a series of disputes, Egil finds himself in the king's disfavor. Instead of fleeing or cowering, Egil composes a powerful poem, the *Höfuðlausn* (Head Ransom), to save his life. His willingness to face danger head-on, combined with his skill in crafting a poem that moved even his enemy, showcases the bravery and honor that define drengskapr.

Grettir the Strong

Grettir the Strong, the protagonist of *Grettir's Saga*, is another legendary figure who exemplifies the Norse ideals of drengskapr. Grettir's life is marked by a series of challenges and adversities, from battling supernatural creatures to surviving years as an outlaw. Despite these hardships, Grettir remains true to his principles, demonstrating courage, resilience, and a sense of justice.

One of the most poignant moments in Grettir's saga is his battle with the draugr (a type of undead creature) Glam. Grettir takes on this fearsome opponent not just for glory but to rid a farmstead of its terror. The fight is brutal, and although Grettir ultimately triumphs, he is cursed by Glam, leading to a life of misfortune. Yet, Grettir never wavers in his resolve to face whatever fate throws at him, embodying the endurance and honor central to drengskapr.

The Legacy of Drengskapr

Both Egil and Grettir, with their flaws and strengths, reflect the Norse ideal of drengskapr. They are not perfect heroes; their sagas show them as individuals who struggle with their inner demons, make mistakes, and face the consequences of their actions. However, it is their commitment to honor, their bravery in the face of overwhelming odds, and their loyalty to their values and loved ones that make them timeless examples of drengskapr.

In the sagas, drengskapr is not just about physical strength or martial prowess; it is about the moral fortitude to do what is right, even when it is difficult or dangerous. The tales of Egil Skallagrimsson and Grettir the Strong continue to inspire readers with their powerful depictions of what it means to live with honor and courage.

The Role of Warfare in Viking Society

Warfare was not just a means of conflict but a way of life for the Vikings. Raiding and conquest were essential for acquiring wealth, resources, and status. Successful warriors gained not only material riches but also social prestige and influence. The spoils of war, including land, slaves, and treasures, contributed to the prosperity of their communities and reinforced the hierarchical structure of Viking society.

The Viking raids, known as vikingr, were organized expeditions involving fleets of longships. These raids targeted monasteries, towns, and coastal settlements across Europe, taking advantage of the element of surprise and the Vikings' superior seafaring capabilities. The wealth acquired from these raids funded further expeditions and the establishment of settlements, such as those in Iceland, Greenland, and even North America.

Apart from raiding, Vikings also participated in large-scale battles and wars, often working as mercenaries or forming alliances with other rulers. Their reputation as fierce and formidable fighters made them sought-after allies and feared adversaries. The use of berserkers, warriors who fought in a trance-like fury, added to their fearsome reputation and effectiveness in battle.

Honor in battle was paramount for the Vikings. A warrior's reputation was built on their bravery and conduct in combat. Acts of valor and skill were celebrated, while cowardice and dishonor were condemned. The bond between warriors was sacred, and fighting alongside one's comrades was both a duty and a source of pride.

The importance of honor extended to the treatment of enemies. While Vikings were known for their ruthless tactics, they also respected the concept of honorable combat. Surrendered foes could be spared and incorporated into the victor's ranks or ransomed for wealth. The treatment of captives varied, but those who demonstrated bravery could earn respect, even in defeat.

The rituals surrounding battle, such as weapon blessings and oaths of loyalty, reinforced the spiritual and cultural significance of warfare. These rituals invoked the favor of the gods and ensured that warriors entered battle with divine support. Victory in battle was seen as a sign of the gods' favor, further validating the warrior's honor and status.

The emphasis on warfare and honor had a profound impact on Viking culture, shaping their social structures, values, and daily lives. The warrior ethos permeated all aspects of society, from the sagas and poetry that celebrated heroic deeds to the rituals and customs that reinforced communal bonds and individual identity.

The legacy of Viking warfare and honor continues to captivate modern imaginations, symbolizing the enduring appeal of courage, loyalty, and the indomitable spirit. The tales of Viking warriors and their exploits remain a testament to the cultural significance of warfare in shaping the identity and history of the Norse people.

In summary, warfare and honor were integral to Viking life, with the concept of *drengskapr* defining the values and conduct expected of a warrior. The glorification of martial prowess, the importance of honorable conduct, and the cultural rituals surrounding battle all contributed to the unique warrior ethos that defined Viking society. These elements, deeply rooted in their mythology and daily practices, continue to resonate through the legacy of the Vikings and their enduring influence on history and culture.

The Berserkers

Fierce warriors, known as berserkers, played a significant role in Viking battles, embodying the raw, unrestrained power of the Norse warrior ethos. These formidable fighters were believed to channel the fury of Odin, the chief of the gods and the god of war, wisdom, and *death*. Berserkers fought in a trance-like state, displaying extraordinary strength and fearlessness, making their presence on the battlefield both inspiring and terrifying.

The term "berserker" likely originates from the Old Norse words "berr" (bear) and "serkr" (shirt), suggesting that these warriors fought in bear skins or even without armor. Alternatively, it could derive from "bare-shirt," indicating that they entered battle without protective clothing, symbolizing their invulnerability and sheer ferocity. Berserkers were often associated with the animalistic attributes of bears and wolves, embodying their strength, aggression, and primal instincts.

Berserkers were believed to possess supernatural abilities granted by the gods, particularly Odin. They were said to enter a state of ecstatic fury, known as "berserkergang," during which they became immune to pain and exhibited near-superhuman strength. In this trance-like state, berserkers were capable of extraordinary feats, such as tearing enemies apart with their bare hands and enduring severe injuries without faltering.

Berserkers were the shock troops of Viking armies, leading the charge into battle and striking fear into the hearts of their enemies. Their frenzied assault could break enemy lines and create chaos, giving the Viking forces a significant advantage. The sight of berserkers, with their wild eyes and blood-curdling screams, often caused opponents to flee in terror, demoralizing entire armies before the main battle even began.

Berserkers' tactical use was not limited to their physical prowess. Their reputation as invincible warriors spread far and wide, serving as a psychological weapon. Stories of their exploits were enough to unsettle foes and weaken their resolve. In addition to their roles as frontline fighters, berserkers also served as bodyguards for chieftains and kings, their loyalty and ferocity ensuring the protection of their leaders.

Berserkers held a special place in Viking culture and mythology, symbolizing the unbridled power and raw courage highly valued in Norse society. They were often depicted in sagas and poems as legendary figures, their deeds celebrated, and their strength revered. The image of the berserker captured the essence of the Viking warrior spirit: fearless, relentless, and indomitable.

Mythologically, berserkers were linked to the god Odin, who was known to bestow his warriors with the ability to enter berserkergang. This divine connection elevated berserkers beyond mere mortals, aligning them with the forces of chaos and transformation that Odin himself embodied. The frenzied state of berserkergang was seen as a gift from the gods, a manifestation of divine power channeled through human vessels.

While the berserkergang conferred immense power, it also had its drawbacks. Berserkers, once in their frenzied state, could become uncontrollable, posing a danger to friend and foe alike. The aftermath of their rage often left them physically and mentally exhausted, vulnerable to counterattacks. This uncontrollable nature made them as much a liability as an asset on the battlefield.

In everyday life, the berserker rage could lead to social and personal challenges. Berserkers were often viewed with a mix of awe and fear by their own communities, their unpredictable behavior making them difficult to integrate into normal social structures. The duality of their existence—heroes in battle but potential threats in peace—reflects the complex nature of their role in Viking society.

Both historical texts and archaeological evidence support the existence of berserkers. Written accounts from the Viking Age, such as the sagas and the writings of medieval historians like Snorri Sturluson, describe the berserkers and their fearsome abilities in vivid detail. These sources provide insights into the cultural significance and legendary status of berserkers.

Archaeological findings, including graves containing weapons and bear pelts, suggest the presence of warriors who may have been berserkers. These artifacts, coupled with depictions of berserkers in runestones and carvings, contribute to our understanding of their role and importance in Viking society. The combination of literary and material evidence paints a picture of berserkers as both historical figures and mythological symbols.

The legacy of the berserkers endures in modern culture, where they are often portrayed in literature, films, and games as the quintessential warriors of Norse mythology. Their image has become synonymous with untamed strength and fearless combat, capturing the imagination of audiences worldwide. The concept of the berserker has transcended its historical origins, becoming a universal symbol of the warrior spirit.

In contemporary interpretations, berserkers are often depicted as tragic heroes, their immense power balanced by the curse of uncontrollable rage. This nuanced portrayal reflects the ongoing fascination with the duality of their nature: the fine line between heroism and monstrosity, order and chaos. The enduring appeal of berserkers lies in their ability to embody the eternal struggle between these opposing forces.

In summary, berserkers were formidable warriors whose frenzied state of berserkergang made them both awe-inspiring and terrifying figures in Viking battles. Their role in warfare, cultural significance, and connection to the divine illustrate the complexity of the Viking warrior ethos. The legacy of the berserkers continues to captivate modern audiences, symbolizing the timeless allure of the untamed warrior spirit.

The Role of the Shieldmaiden

Contrary to the male-dominated view of warfare, Norse mythology and sagas mention shieldmaidens—women who took up arms and fought alongside men. These female warriors were celebrated for their bravery, skill, and leadership in battle, challenging contemporary gender norms and highlighting the inclusive nature of Viking warrior culture.

Figures of Legend

Lagertha, a legendary figure in Norse history and mythology, is renowned as a fierce warrior, a skilled shieldmaiden, and the wife of the famous Viking leader Ragnar Lothbrok. Her story, though interwoven with myth and historical uncertainty, is a testament to the strength and prowess of women in Viking society. Lagertha's tale is primarily recounted in the "Gesta

Danorum" (Deeds of the Danes), a 12th-century work by the Danish historian Saxo Grammaticus.

Lagertha's story begins with a tragedy and a call to arms. According to the legends, the Norwegian chieftain Frø invaded Sweden, killed the king, and placed the women of the royal family in a brothel for public humiliation. Ragnar Lothbrok, a young warrior and future king, sought to avenge this outrage. He gathered an army to liberate the women and exact justice on Frø.

It was during this campaign that Ragnar encountered Lagertha, who had disguised herself as a man to join the fight. She was described as a woman with a valiant spirit and incredible martial skills. Lagertha's bravery and strength in battle stood out, as she fought alongside the men and played a crucial role in Ragnar's victory over Frø. Her prowess in combat earned her the respect and admiration of Ragnar and his warriors.

Impressed by her courage and beauty, Ragnar pursued Lagertha as a potential wife. However, their courtship was not without challenges. Saxo Grammaticus recounts that when Ragnar came to court Lagertha, she initially tested his resolve by setting a bear and a large hound upon him. Undeterred, Ragnar killed the animals and won Lagertha's hand in marriage.

Together, Ragnar and Lagertha had children, including a son named Fridleif and two daughters. Their marriage, however, was not destined to last. The reasons for their separation vary, with some accounts suggesting it was due to Ragnar's ambitions and infidelities. Despite their parting, Lagertha continued to be a formidable figure in her own right.

After separating from Ragnar, Lagertha returned to Norway, where she ruled as a queen in her own right. Her story doesn't end with her marriage to Ragnar; instead, she continued to lead and inspire as a warrior and leader.

One notable episode later in her life involved her coming to Ragnar's aid. When Ragnar was embroiled in a civil war with his former ally and current rival, King Eysteinn of Sweden, he found himself in a precarious situation. Lagertha, demonstrating her enduring loyalty and warrior spirit, came to his rescue. She arrived with a fleet and a force of warriors, playing a pivotal role in turning the tide of battle in Ragnar's favor.

In a surprising twist, Saxo Grammaticus also notes that Lagertha's story ended on a darker note. After returning to Norway, she reportedly killed her then-husband with a spearhead concealed in her gown, taking control of his kingdom. The motives for this act are not clearly stated, but it highlights her complex character and determination to maintain her power and autonomy.

Lagertha's legend has persisted through the centuries, capturing the imagination of many. She represents the archetype of the shieldmaiden— women who fought alongside men in battle and held positions of power and influence. While the historical accuracy of her life is debated, with some scholars questioning the existence of shieldmaidens in Viking society, Lagertha's story has become an enduring symbol of female strength and resilience.

In modern times, Lagertha has been popularized through various media, most notably in the television series "Vikings," where she is portrayed as a central character, blending historical elements with mythological and dramatic interpretations. This portrayal has further solidified her status as an iconic figure representing the warrior spirit and the empowerment of women.

Lagertha's story is a powerful narrative of courage, independence, and the complexities of leadership. Her legacy continues to inspire, reminding us of the diverse and dynamic roles women have played throughout history and mythology.

The Story of Hervor

The story of Hervor is a compelling tale from the *Hervarar saga*, a Norse saga that intertwines elements of myth, legend, and history. Hervor is renowned as a shieldmaiden, a woman who defies the traditional gender roles of her time by taking up arms and pursuing a warrior's path. Her journey is centered around reclaiming the cursed sword Tyrfing, a legendary weapon with a dark history, and it reflects the values of courage, determination, and honor that were celebrated in Viking culture.

The saga begins with the history of the sword Tyrfing, which was forged by dwarves under duress and cursed to bring misfortune and death to its bearer. The sword was originally owned by Angantyr, a mighty warrior and Hervor's father, who died along with his brothers in a duel on the island of Samsø. The sword was buried with Angantyr, and it was said to be guarded by a ghostly presence, as the dead warrior and his brothers had been denied peace due to the curse.

Hervor was raised in ignorance of her lineage and the cursed legacy of Tyrfing. However, as she grew older, she learned of her father's fate and the existence of the powerful sword. Driven by a desire to reclaim her family's honor and assert her warrior heritage, Hervor disguised herself as a man, taking on the name Hervardr, and set out on a quest to retrieve Tyrfing.

Her journey took her to the island of Samsø, where she ventured into the burial mound of her father and uncles. There, she encountered their restless spirits. In a scene filled with supernatural tension, Hervor fearlessly confronted the shades of the dead, demanding that they surrender the sword to her. The ghost of Angantyr warned her of the sword's curse, foretelling the doom it would bring, but Hervor was undeterred. Her courage and determination prevailed, and she successfully claimed Tyrfing.

Despite the warnings, Hervor was resolute in her desire to wield Tyrfing. She left Samsø with the sword, becoming a formidable warrior in her own right. However, the curse of Tyrfing soon became evident. The

119

sword, though incredibly powerful and always sharp, could not be drawn without taking a life. It brought tragedy and conflict wherever it went.

Hervor's story continues with her son, Heidrek, who inherits Tyrfing. The curse of the sword brings further misfortune, leading to betrayal and bloodshed within their family. The saga recounts the ongoing struggle with the sword's dark legacy, as each subsequent wielder grapples with its malevolent power.

Hervor's story is significant not only for her bravery and warrior spirit but also for the themes it explores. The saga delves into the complexities of fate, honor, and the consequences of wielding great power. Hervor's determination to reclaim Tyrfing and assert her identity as a warrior highlights the values of courage and resilience in the face of daunting challenges.

The *Hervarar saga* presents Hervor as a complex and multi-faceted character. She defies traditional gender roles by embracing the life of a warrior, and she confronts the supernatural without fear. Her quest for Tyrfing and the subsequent challenges she faces emphasize the high price of pursuing glory and the heavy burden of carrying a cursed legacy.

Hervor's tale has resonated through the ages, illustrating the rich narrative tradition of Norse sagas and the portrayal of strong, determined women in Viking lore. Her story, like those of other legendary shieldmaidens, challenges modern perceptions of gender roles in the Viking Age and celebrates the indomitable spirit of those who sought to define their own destinies in a world governed by fate and honor.

While the accounts of shieldmaidens in sagas and legends are compelling, archaeological evidence also supports the existence of female warriors in Viking society. Graves containing weapons and warrior artifacts have been discovered, suggesting that some women were buried with the same honors as their male counterparts. These findings indicate that women did participate in combat and were recognized for their contributions.

The existence of shieldmaidens challenges the traditional narrative of Viking warfare as exclusively male and highlights the complex social dynamics of the time. These women fought in battles and held leadership roles, demonstrating their capacity for strategy and command.

Including shieldmaidens in Norse mythology and sagas underscores the value placed on bravery, regardless of gender. The stories of Lagertha, Hervor, and others were powerful narratives that inspired and validated women's roles in Viking society. They exemplified the belief that heroism and strength were not confined to men and that women could also achieve great deeds and honor. Shieldmaidens symbolize the broader cultural ideals of the Vikings, where personal valor and honor were paramount. Their tales continue to inspire modern interpretations of female warriors, reinforcing the timeless appeal of their strength and courage.

Honor and reputation were paramount in Viking society, and these values were often upheld through oaths and feuds. Oaths sworn before the gods were considered inviolable, binding individuals to their word with the threat of divine retribution for those who broke them. Feuds, on the other hand, were common and could escalate into cycles of revenge that defined social and legal interactions.

In Viking culture, oaths were solemn promises made before the gods and the community. These oaths were taken seriously, as breaking them was believed to invoke the wrath of the gods and bring dishonor upon the individual and their family. Oaths were used to forge alliances, settle disputes, and affirm commitments, ensuring trust and stability within the society.

The importance of oaths is reflected in the sagas, where characters frequently swear oaths of loyalty, revenge, or peace. Breaking an oath had severe consequences, often resulting in social ostracism or violent retribution. This cultural emphasis on the sanctity of oaths reinforced the value of personal honor and integrity.

The sagas are replete with stories of feuds, illustrating the complexities of Viking justice and the importance of reputation. One famous example is the feud between the families of Njáll Þorgeirsson and Flosi Þórðarson in the Njáls saga. The feud between the families of Njáll Þorgeirsson and Flosi Þórðarson, as detailed in the *Njáls saga*, is one of the most dramatic and tragic narratives in Icelandic literature. The saga, also known as the *Story of Burnt Njáll*, is one of the longest and most complex of the Icelandic sagas, blending legal disputes, honor codes, and the consequences of vengeance in a vividly portrayed medieval Icelandic society.

The roots of the feud can be traced to a series of complex personal and legal disputes. One key figure in the saga is Njáll Þorgeirsson, a wise and respected chieftain known for his legal acumen and peaceful nature. He was married to Bergþóra, a strong-willed woman. Njáll's friend and foster brother, Gunnar Hámundarson, is a heroic warrior, whose tragic end begins to set the stage for the feud.

After Gunnar's death, his enemies are left without direct vengeance due to Njáll's mediation. However, tension arises between Njáll's family and other powerful figures, including the influential chieftain Flosi Þórðarson. The immediate cause of the feud starts with a complicated series of events involving Njáll's sons and Flosi's extended family.

One of the critical incidents sparking the feud involves Höskuldr Hvítanessgoði, a respected goði (chieftain) and a relative of Flosi. Njáll, demonstrating his wisdom and kindness, adopts Höskuldr as a foster son, and the young man becomes dear to him. However, a rivalry develops between

122

Höskuldr and Njáll's biological sons, particularly Þorgerður and Skarphedinn.

The situation escalates when Njáll's sons, driven by jealousy and goaded by their mother Bergþóra, ambush and kill Höskuldr while he is working in his field. This act of treachery is particularly heinous because Höskuldr had been at peace with Njáll's family, and the killing is seen as both cowardly and dishonorable. Njáll, deeply saddened by the murder, tries to offer compensation for the slaying, but the offer is seen as inadequate by Höskuldr's kin.

Flosi Þórðarson, Höskuldr's uncle and a powerful chieftain, becomes the leader of those seeking vengeance. Flosi is portrayed as a formidable and shrewd leader, capable of both compassion and ruthlessness. He gathers a coalition of supporters to avenge Höskuldr's death. The legal attempts to resolve the matter fail, primarily due to the complexities of Icelandic law and the influence of the involved families.

As tensions escalate, Flosi decides on a brutal course of action. He gathers a large group of men, intending to burn Njáll and his family alive in their home at Bergþórshvoll, as a means of exacting revenge.

Flosi and his men lay siege to Njáll's farm in one of the most harrowing scenes in Icelandic literature. As the saga recounts, Njáll, now an elderly man, and his wife Bergþóra choose to stay inside their burning house with their grandson, refusing to leave. Njáll believes that if he is meant to die, it is better to meet death with dignity. His sons fight valiantly, but the overwhelming force and fire consume the household. Only Kári Sölmundarson, Njáll's son-in-law, manages to escape the blaze.

The burning of Njáll and his family is a turning point in the saga, representing a profound breach of the moral and legal codes of Icelandic society. The act horrifies many, including some of Flosi's own men, who regret their participation in such a gruesome event. The aftermath of the burning leads to further violence and retribution. Kári, one of the survivors, embarks on a quest for revenge against the burners, killing many of them in single combat and skirmishes. The saga details Kári's relentless pursuit of justice and vengeance, which brings him into direct conflict with Flosi and his supporters.

However, as time passes, both parties grow weary of the bloodshed. The saga culminates in a reconciliation at the Alþingi (the Icelandic assembly), where Flosi and Kári agree to a settlement. Flosi's public display of remorse, his confession, and the payment of wergild (compensation) help to restore peace. The saga ends with Kári and Flosi making peace, symbolizing the complex nature of honor, vengeance, and reconciliation in Viking society.

The *Njáls saga* explores the devastating effects of blood feuds and the difficulties of balancing justice and mercy. It portrays a society in transition, grappling with the old ways of honor and vengeance and the emerging need for legal resolution and peace. The saga also delves into the themes of fate, honor, and the consequences of violence. Njáll's character, embodying wisdom and a desire for peace, stands in stark contrast to the destructive forces of vengeance that dominate the narrative. The tragic end of Njáll and his family serves as a cautionary tale about the dangers of unrestrained revenge and the importance of law and reconciliation.

The *Njáls saga* remains one of the most significant works in Icelandic literature, offering deep insights into the values, social structures, and conflicts of medieval Iceland. Its enduring legacy continues to influence Icelandic culture and literature, as well as our understanding of Viking-age society.

This feud, marked by a series of retaliatory killings, highlights the enduring nature of such conflicts and the lengths to which individuals would go to defend their honor.

Cultural Reflection

The interplay between oaths and feuds in Viking society reflects the broader cultural values of honor, loyalty, and justice. The emphasis on keeping one's word and avenging wrongs highlights the importance of personal and familial reputation.

In summary, the roles of shieldmaidens, the sanctity of oaths, and the cycle of feuds all contribute to our understanding of Viking culture. These elements illustrate the complexity of social interactions and the importance of honor and reputation in shaping the lives of the Norse people. The stories and practices associated with these aspects continue to captivate and inspire, offering insights into a society where valor and integrity were paramount.

Agriculture and Craftsmanship

While the Vikings were often celebrated for their raiding and exploration, they were also highly skilled farmers, traders, and craftsmen. These aspects of their daily lives were deeply intertwined with their mythology, reflecting their connection to the land and their artisanal expertise.

Agriculture: The Backbone of Viking Society

Agriculture was the backbone of Viking society, essential for sustaining their communities and supporting their way of life. Viking farmers were adept at cultivating the land, growing crops such as barley, oats, and rye, which were staples of their diet. They also raised livestock, including cattle, sheep, pigs, and goats, providing meat, dairy products, and wool.

Rituals and Beliefs: The Vikings invoked the blessings of gods like Freyr and Thor for bountiful harvests. Freyr, the god of fertility and agriculture, was particularly revered during planting and harvest times. Rituals included offerings of the first fruits and sacrifices to ensure fertility and protect against natural disasters. Thor, with his association with storms and rain, was also called upon to safeguard crops from adverse weather.

Seasonal Festivals: Agricultural cycles were marked by seasonal festivals, such as Yule, a midwinter celebration that honored the rebirth of the sun and the god Balder. These festivals included feasts, sacrifices, and communal gatherings, reinforcing social bonds and ensuring the favor of the gods for the coming year. These celebrations were not only times of communal joy but also reinforced the Vikings' reliance on divine favor for agricultural success.

Daily Life and Labor

Farming was a communal effort involving the entire household. Men, women, and children all played roles in planting, tending, and harvesting crops. The labor-intensive nature of agriculture fostered a strong sense of community and interdependence. The cyclical rhythm of the farming year was mirrored in the mythology, with its themes of growth, death, and renewal.

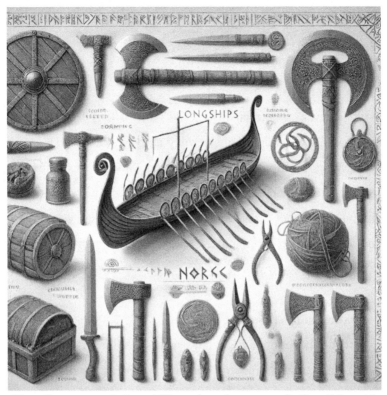

Craftsmanship: The Artisans of the North

The Vikings were renowned for their craftsmanship, excelling in metalwork, woodwork, textiles, and shipbuilding. Their artisanal skills were practical and a source of artistic expression, with intricate designs and patterns that reflected their cultural heritage.

Metalwork and Jewelry

Viking metalworkers created a wide range of items, from weapons and tools to jewelry and ornaments. Their craftsmanship in forging swords, axes, and spears was highly regarded, with some pieces becoming legendary, such as Sigmund's sword Gram. Jewelry, often made of silver and gold, featured intricate designs, including animal motifs and interlacing patterns.

These items were both decorative and symbolic, often serving as status symbols and protective charms.

Woodwork and Carving

Wood was a primary material for Viking artisans, used in constructing buildings, ships, and everyday items. Viking woodworkers were skilled in carving, creating detailed designs on wooden chests, furniture, and ship prows. The art of carving extended to runestones, which were erected to commemorate important events and individuals. These stones, inscribed with runes and adorned with carvings, served as lasting testaments to the Viking legacy.

Textiles and Weaving

Textile production was a vital aspect of Viking craftsmanship, with women primarily responsible for spinning, weaving, and dyeing fabrics. Wool and flax were the main materials used to produce clothing, blankets, and sails for ships. The process of weaving was labor-intensive and required great skill, resulting in high-quality textiles that were both functional and beautiful.

Shipbuilding

Perhaps the most iconic aspect of Viking craftsmanship was their shipbuilding. The longships, with their sleek design and shallow draught, were marvels of engineering, allowing the Vikings to navigate both open seas and shallow rivers. These ships were crucial for their raiding, trading, and exploration activities, symbolizing the Vikings' adventurous spirit and technological prowess. The construction of a longship was a communal effort, often involving the entire community in gathering materials and assembling the vessel.

Trade and Commerce

The Vikings were not only raiders but also prolific traders, establishing extensive trade networks that spanned from the North Atlantic to the Mediterranean and beyond. Their craftsmanship played a significant role in their commercial success, with Viking goods highly sought after in foreign markets.

Trade Routes and Centers: Viking trade routes extended across Europe and into Asia, connecting them with distant civilizations. Major trade centers, such as Birka in Sweden, Hedeby in Denmark, and Dublin in Ireland, became bustling hubs of commerce. These centers facilitated the exchange of goods, including furs, amber, textiles, and metalwork, for exotic items like spices, silk, and silver.

Cultural Exchange

Through trade, the Vikings encountered diverse cultures and technologies, which they assimilated and adapted. This cultural exchange enriched Viking society, leading to innovations in their craftsmanship and the incorporation of new styles and techniques. The blending of indigenous and foreign elements is evident in Viking art and artifacts, showcasing their ability to adapt and innovate.

Economic Impact

Trade significantly boosted the Viking economy, providing wealth and resources that fueled further expansion and exploration. The prosperity gained from commerce allowed for the development of settlements, the construction of monumental structures, and the patronage of artisans and craftsmen. This economic foundation supported the Viking way of life, enabling them to thrive in a challenging environment.

131

Mythological Reflections

Viking mythology reflects their connection to the land and their craftsmanship. The gods themselves were often depicted as craftsmen and laborers. Thor, for example, was not only the god of thunder but also a protector of farmers. Freyr, associated with fertility and prosperity, was invoked for both agricultural success and trade. The myths conveyed the importance of hard work, ingenuity, and the respect for natural cycles, mirroring the daily experiences of the Viking people.

Mythical Artisans

Figures like the dwarves in Norse mythology were master craftsmen, creating some of the most powerful and significant items in the mythos, such as Thor's hammer Mjölnir and Odin's spear Gungnir. These mythical artisans represented the ideal of craftsmanship, embodying skill, creativity, and the magical properties of their creations.

Rituals and Offerings

Rituals often involved offerings of crafted items, such as weapons and jewelry, to the gods. These offerings were believed to curry favor and ensure divine protection and prosperity. Crafting and offering these items was a form of devotion, emphasizing the sacred nature of their work and the connection between craftsmanship and spirituality.

Agriculture and craftsmanship were integral to Viking society, deeply influencing their daily lives and cultural identity. Their mythology reflected their connection to the land and their artisanal skills and provided a framework for understanding and honoring these essential aspects of their existence. The Vikings' ability to cultivate the land, create intricate works of art, and engage in extensive trade networks underscores their adaptability and resilience, qualities that continue to fascinate and inspire today.

The Role of the Chieftain

Chieftains were pivotal figures in Viking society, holding secular and religious authority. They led their people in battle, presided over rituals, and acted as judges and lawmakers. The chieftain's power was substantial but balanced by the thing, ensuring that even common men had a voice in community matters.

Secular Authority

Chieftains were responsible for maintaining order and protecting their communities. They led warriors in battles and raids, making strategic decisions that affected the survival and prosperity of their people. Their leadership extended to the administration of justice and the enforcement of laws, reflecting the importance of a strong and just leader in Viking culture.

Religious Authority

In addition to their secular duties, chieftains also presided over religious rituals and ceremonies. They acted as intermediaries between the gods and their people, offering sacrifices and leading festivals to ensure divine favor. This dual role reinforced the chieftain's position as a central figure in both the spiritual and temporal aspects of Viking life.

Balance of Power

Despite their authority, chieftains' power was checked by the thing, a democratic assembly where free men could express their opinions and vote on important matters. This system ensured that decisions were made with the consent of the community, reflecting the Norse values of fairness and collective responsibility.

Legal Practices

Viking law was based on customs and traditions, passed down orally through generations. The legal system emphasized community involvement, fairness, and consensus, providing a structured way to resolve conflicts and administer justice.

Oral Tradition

Laws were not written but memorized and recited by legal experts known as law speakers. These individuals played a crucial role in preserving and interpreting the law, ensuring that it remained consistent and adaptable to changing circumstances.

Legal Assemblies

The thing served as a platform for resolving disputes and making legal decisions. It was a gathering where free men could present their cases, seek justice, and participate in the legislative process. Legal assemblies were held at local, regional, and national levels, with the Althing in Iceland being one of the most famous examples.

Dispute Resolution

Conflicts were often settled through negotiation and mediation at the thing. If a resolution could not be reached, trials were held where evidence and testimonies were presented. The emphasis was on finding a fair and equitable solution that upheld the community's values and norms.

Punishments and Compensation

Punishments for crimes varied but often involved compensation to the victim or their family, known as wergild. This system of restitution aimed to restore balance and prevent further violence, reflecting the Norse emphasis on maintaining social harmony.

Women's Rights

Compared to other contemporary cultures, Viking women enjoyed relatively more rights and freedoms. Norse mythology, with its powerful female figures, mirrored and reinforced the respect and agency that women held in Viking society.

Property Rights

Viking women could own and manage property, including land, livestock, and household goods. This economic independence allowed them to participate actively in the community and contributed to their social status.

Marriage and Divorce

Women had the right to request a divorce if they were unhappy in their marriage. They could reclaim their dowries and return to their families, providing a measure of security and autonomy. Marriage was often viewed as a partnership, with women playing crucial roles in managing households and estates.

Legal Standing

Women could represent themselves in legal matters and participate in the thing. They could bring lawsuits, defend their rights, and seek justice, highlighting their active role in the legal system. Although their participation was not on equal footing with men, it was significant compared to other societies of the time.

Influence of Mythology

Norse mythology featured strong female figures, such as Freyja, the goddess of love and war, and the Norns, who controlled fate. These deities embodied power, wisdom, and independence, reflecting the societal values that allowed Viking women to hold respected and influential positions.

Cultural Reflection

The Viking social structure and legal practices were deeply influenced by their mythology, reflecting the values of honor, fairness, and community. The dual role of chieftains as both leaders and religious figures underscored the integration of spiritual and temporal authority. The democratic nature of the thing demonstrated the importance of collective decision-making and the respect for individual voices within the community.

The relative rights and freedoms of Viking women, mirrored by the powerful female figures in their mythology, highlight a society that valued and respected the contributions of all its members. These aspects of Viking life provide a nuanced understanding of their culture, showcasing a complex and dynamic society where law, honor, and mythology were intricately intertwined.

In summary, the social structure and legal system of the Vikings were shaped by their mythology and cultural values. The role of the chieftain, the practices of the thing, and the rights of women all reflected a society that prized fairness, honor, and community involvement. These elements contributed to the resilience and cohesion of Viking communities, allowing them to thrive in a challenging environment and leaving a lasting legacy that continues to fascinate and inspire today.

Consider the interplay between myth and reality, exploring how stories shaped societal norms and individual behaviors. Norse mythology was not just a reflection of Viking life but a guide for living, offering lessons on bravery, honor, and the importance of community.

Now that we have delved into the intersection of Norse mythology and Viking culture, reflect on how these ancient beliefs and practices resonate with modern values. Consider how mythology shapes our understanding of history and identity. Let the stories of the gods and the practices of the Vikings inspire you to explore the rich cultural heritage that continues to influence our world today.

Chapter 5:

Magic and Runes

Enter the mystical world of Norse magic, where ancient runes hold the secrets of the cosmos and the practice of seidr weaves the intricate threads of fate. In the Viking Age, magic was not merely a set of rituals or spells but an integral part of daily life, deeply intertwined with the people's understanding of the universe and their place within it. The Norse believed the visible world was just one layer of reality, coexisting with unseen realms inhabited by gods, spirits, and other supernatural beings.

Runes were more than just an alphabet; they were symbols imbued with powerful magical significance. Each rune represented not only a sound but also possessed inherent meanings connected to natural elements, emotions, and divine forces. Carving runes onto weapons, jewelry, or stones was a sacred practice intended to invoke protection, strength, or favorable outcomes in battle and daily endeavors. Runes were also used in divination practices, where seers would interpret their meanings to provide guidance, predict the future, or uncover hidden truths, reflecting the Vikings' desire to understand and influence the forces that shaped their lives.

The practice of seidr, a form of Norse magic associated primarily with prophecy and altering the course of destiny, was another crucial aspect of their mystical traditions. Practiced by seeresses known as völvas and sometimes by gods like Odin and Freyja, seidr involved rituals that could manipulate the elements, communicate with the spirit world, or alter one's luck. These rituals often included chanting, drumming, and entering trance-like states to traverse different realms of existence. Seidr was both respected and feared, highlighting the complex attitudes toward magic and those who wielded it.

The Vikings' beliefs in the supernatural were deeply woven into their social structures, laws, and customs, guiding their actions and providing a framework for understanding the world around them. Omens, dreams, and natural phenomena were interpreted as messages from the gods or otherworldly beings, influencing decisions from personal relationships to matters of war and exploration. Rituals and offerings were made to deities and spirits to ensure favorable outcomes, safe voyages, and bountiful harvests, showcasing a reciprocal relationship between the mortal and divine.

By immersing ourselves in these ancient practices, we gain a deeper appreciation for how magic was not just a belief system but a lens through which the Vikings viewed every aspect of existence. The interplay between the natural and the supernatural in Norse culture reflects a worldview where the boundaries between worlds were permeable, and humans could engage with and influence the spiritual forces around them. This exploration reveals a civilization rich in tradition and spirituality, whose legacy fascinates and inspires our modern understanding of myth and magic.

The Magical Functions of Runes

Beyond their use as a script, runes were believed to hold intrinsic magical properties. The ancient Norse people regarded runes not merely as letters for recording language but as potent symbols imbued with mystical energies. Each rune encapsulated a specific power or concept, allowing practitioners to tap into and influence the world around them. The runic alphabet, known as the Elder Futhark, consisted of 24 characters, each associated with cosmic forces, deities, and elements of nature. For instance, the rune Fehu symbolized wealth and prosperity, Uruz represented strength and vitality, and Algiz was linked to protection and defense.

Practitioners of runic magic, often called rune masters or rune magicians, were individuals skilled in interpreting and harnessing these symbols' powers. They believed that they could invoke the desired effects by inscribing runes with intention and performing specific rituals. Carving runes was considered a sacred act, requiring focus, precision, and a deep understanding of the runes' meanings.

Runes were used in various forms of magic and ritual, permeating many aspects of Viking life. Warriors might inscribe runes onto their swords and shields to ensure protection and victory in battle. Such inscriptions strengthened the weapon and imbued the warrior with courage and might. Farmers sought to ensure fertility and abundant harvests by carving runes onto their tools or barn doors, invoking the favor of deities like Freyr, the god of fertility.

Runes also ward off evil spirits and negative energies. Amulets and talismans bearing protective runes were commonly worn or placed in homes to safeguard against harm. In healing practices, specific runes were used in rituals intended to cure ailments and restore health. Conversely, runes could be employed in curses or bindings against enemies, reflecting their versatility and the belief in their inherent power.

Runic divination was another significant aspect. Runemasters cast rune stones or sticks and interpreted the symbols to guide decisions, predict future events, or gain insight into hidden matters. This practice reflects the deep connection between the runes and the spiritual realm, highlighting their importance in Norse culture as tools for communication with the divine.

Runes in Daily Life

The integration of runes into daily Viking life underscores their significance as magical tools and as essential means of communication and expression. Runes were carved on monuments like the numerous runestones in Scandinavia. These stones often commemorated notable individuals, events, or journeys and were lasting tributes to ancestors' deeds. The inscriptions combined factual records with expressions of honor and remembrance, bridging the mortal and spiritual worlds.

Runes served both practical and mystical purposes on weapons and armor. A sword might bear runes calling for victory, strength, or the favor of gods like Odin or Tyr. Shields could be inscribed with protective runes to ward off enemy blows. This practice highlights the Vikings' belief in the tangible influence of runic magic on the battlefield, where physical prowess was augmented by spiritual empowerment.

Runes were used to bring blessings or functionality to everyday objects. Household items like bowls, combs, and tools might be decorated with runic inscriptions to ensure prosperity, happiness, or protection for the family. Ships, vital for exploration and trade, often bore runes carved into their hulls or masts to secure safe passage across treacherous seas. Merchants might use runes to guard their goods or invoke success in trade.

Amulets and talismans were commonly worn by individuals seeking the runes' benefits in personal matters. These could range from love charms to symbols promoting good health or success in endeavors. The personalization of runic inscriptions allowed individuals to carry the power of the runes with them, integrating magic into the fabric of daily existence.

Runes' legal and administrative uses further demonstrate their versatility. Contracts, property marks, and official proclamations were sometimes inscribed in runes, lending authority and permanence to important documents. This dual role as both a practical script and a medium for magical expression highlights the profound respect and significance the Vikings placed on runes.

Preservation and Legacy

The knowledge of runes and their uses was passed down through generations, often safeguarded by skilled rune masters who were both literate and versed in magical practices. These individuals held esteemed societal positions, serving as scribes, storytellers, and spiritual advisors. They played a crucial role in preserving the runic traditions, teaching the meanings and proper uses of each rune to apprentices, and ensuring their continued relevance in an evolving culture.

With the spread of Christianity in Scandinavia, the use of runes faced significant challenges. The new religion discouraged pagan practices, viewing runic magic with suspicion and often associating it with witchcraft. However, runes continued to be used, sometimes covertly, blending with Christian symbols and themes. Some runestones from this period display a fascinating mix of pagan and Christian imagery, reflecting a society in transition.

The enduring fascination with runes is evident in their presence in modern culture. Scholars and enthusiasts have studied runic inscriptions to gain insights into Viking language, society, and beliefs. Runes have been revived in various esoteric practices, including modern paganism and neo-Norse spiritual movements. They are used in contemporary divination and meditation and as symbols in jewelry and art, signifying protection, inspiration, or a connection to ancestral heritage.

The runes' influence extends to literature and popular media, appearing in novels, films, and games inspired by Norse mythology. This ongoing legacy reflects runes' deep-rooted power and mystique within and beyond their original cultural context, highlighting their universal appeal and the timeless human fascination with symbols and magic.

In sum, the power of runes in Norse culture was profound, seamlessly blending the mystical with the every day and offering a vivid example of how spirituality and practicality intertwined in Viking society.

145

The story of Odin's sacrifice for the knowledge of runes is a cornerstone of Norse mythology. According to the myth, Odin hung himself from Yggdrasil, the World Tree, for nine nights, pierced by his own spear, in a self-sacrificial quest to uncover the secrets of the runes. This arduous ordeal granted him profound wisdom and mastery over the runic symbols, emphasizing the immense value placed on knowledge and the lengths one might go to attain it.

The runes remain a testament to the Norse people's quest for understanding and mastery over their world—a quest that continues to captivate our imagination today. Their enduring legacy invites us to explore ancient wisdom, the mysteries of language and symbols, and how culture and belief shape human experience. The runes are not merely historical artifacts but living symbols that continue to inspire, connect, and challenge us to delve deeper into the rich tapestry of our shared heritage. Through the runes, we glimpse a world where magic and reality coalesce, reminding us of the profound connections between the past and the present, the seen and the unseen.

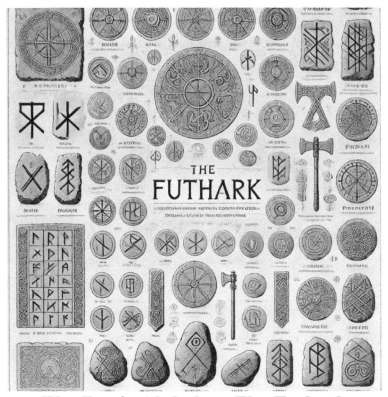

The Runic Alphabet: The Futhark

The Futhark, the ancient runic alphabet used by the Norse and other Germanic peoples, consists of 24 runes, each imbued with its own unique meaning, symbolism, and significance. These runes were more than mere letters; they were potent symbols believed to hold intrinsic magical properties. Carved into materials like wood, stone, bone, and metal, the runes were utilized in various facets of life—including spells, charms, inscriptions, and divination practices.

Each rune was thought to carry inherent magical power, capable of influencing the world around it. Carving a rune was a sacred ritual, often performed with great care and intention. The shapes and symbols of the runes reflect various natural and cosmic forces, embodying the Norse understanding of the universe and its place within it.

The Futhark is divided into three groups, known as aettir (singular: aett), with each aett comprising eight runes. Each aett is associated with different deities and represents various aspects of life and nature:

Freyr's Aett: Associated with fertility, wealth, and prosperity. It includes runes like Fehu (wealth), Uruz (strength), and Thurisaz (giant).

Heimdall's Aett: Connected to human experiences and challenges. Runes like Hagalaz (disruption) and Jera (harvest) belong here.

Tyr's Aett: Linked to justice, victory, and spiritual matters, featuring runes such as Tiwaz (honor) and Dagaz (breakthrough).

The deliberate design of each rune's shape was believed to mirror its metaphysical essence. For instance, Algiz, resembling a person with outstretched arms, symbolized protection and reaching out to the divine, while Sowilo, shaped like a lightning bolt or the sun's rays, represented energy and success.

Divination and Magic

Runes played a crucial role in divination, serving as tools for seeking guidance and insight into the future. Casting runes involved drawing a selection of runes and interpreting their meanings based on their positions, orientations, and relationships to one another. This practice was not solely about foretelling future events but also about understanding the present circumstances and uncovering hidden knowledge.

Casting runes was a ritualistic process, often performed by a seer or runemaster who possessed specialized knowledge of the runes' meanings and magical properties. The practitioner would pose a question or focus on a particular situation, then cast the runes onto a cloth or designated surface. The patterns formed by the runes, along with their individual symbols, were interpreted to provide answers or insights.

Each rune's shape and symbol carried specific meanings:

148

Fehu: Symbolizing cattle and wealth, it represented prosperity and abundance.

Ansuz: Associated with the god Odin, it signified communication, wisdom, and divine inspiration.

Raidho: Depicting a wagon or journey, it embodied travel, movement, and life paths.

Incantations, chants, or prayers often accompanied casting runes to the gods and sometimes included offerings such as mead or other tokens of respect. This sacred practice reinforced the connection between the practitioner, the runes, and the divine forces at work.

Beyond divination, runes were integral to various magical practices and rituals. They were inscribed on amulets for protection, carved into weapons to ensure victory, and used in spells to invoke specific powers or deities. The Norse believed that by inscribing a rune with intention, they could harness its energy to influence outcomes in the physical world.

Amulets and Talismans: Runes like Algiz were commonly used for protection against harm and evil spirits. Warriors might wear amulets with Tiwaz for courage and honor in battle.

Weapons and Armor: Carving runes onto swords, shields, and helmets was believed to enhance their effectiveness. For example, Sowilo might be used to bring success, while Eihwaz could offer strength and resilience.

Magical Spells: Runes were combined into bind runes to create personalized symbols for specific intentions. A bind rune incorporating Gebo (gift) and Wunjo (joy) might be used in love spells or to foster harmonious relationships.

The symbolism of each rune was deeply connected to the natural and supernatural worlds. The runes represented fundamental concepts such as life and death, order and chaos, and the elements of earth, air, fire, and water.

Skilled practitioners understood these connections and could manipulate them through careful selection and arrangement of runes.

Preservation and Legacy

Runemasters and skalds (poets and storytellers) preserved the knowledge and use of runes through oral tradition and the dedicated work of runemasters and skalds. These individuals were both literate and skilled in magical practices, ensuring that runic wisdom was passed down through generations. They played a vital role in maintaining the cultural heritage and spiritual beliefs of the Norse people.

Runestones, large stones engraved with runic inscriptions, served as lasting monuments to significant events, individuals, and beliefs. Found throughout Scandinavia and other regions influenced by the Vikings, these stones often commemorated fallen warriors, marked territorial boundaries, or told stories of voyages and battles. They stand as tangible connections to the past, offering insights into the societal values and practices of the time.

The legacy of the runes continues to this day. Their symbols appear in modern esoteric practices, such as neo-paganism and modern heathenry, where they are used in rituals, meditation, and personal development. Runes have also permeated popular culture, featuring in literature, movies, video games, and artwork inspired by Norse mythology. This enduring fascination reflects a lasting interest in their mystical and historical significance.

Conclusion

With its blend of linguistic and magical functions, the runic alphabet stands as a testament to the Norse people's deep connection to both the mystical and practical aspects of life. The runes provided a means of communication across distances and generations, enabling the recording of history, laws, and poetry. Simultaneously, they served as powerful tools for

magic and divination, allowing individuals to interact with the spiritual realm and seek control over their destinies.

The story of the runes' origin, discovered through Odin's sacrifice, highlights the profound value placed on knowledge and power in Norse mythology. Studied, interpreted, and celebrated, ensuring that the wisdom they carry endures for future generations to explore.

Seidr: The Art of Norse Magic

Seidr is a form of Norse magic associated with prophecy and altering the course of fate. Practiced primarily by women known as völvas, seidr involved trance-like states and communication with the spirit world. This ancient magical practice was a profound aspect of Norse culture, intertwining the realms of the living and the supernatural.

The Practice of Seidr: Seidr practitioners would enter trances, often induced by chanting and drumming, to communicate with spirits and gain insight into the future. These sessions were believed to access hidden knowledge and manipulate fate. The völvas, respected and sometimes feared, wielded considerable power through their ability to foresee and influence events. Their rituals often took place in sacred spaces, where the boundaries between the physical and spiritual worlds were thin. The practice of seidr was both revered and feared, highlighting the powerful and mysterious nature of this magical tradition.

Freyja and Seidr: Freyja, the goddess of love, beauty, and war, is closely associated with seidr. She taught the art to the Aesir, the principal group of gods in Norse mythology, symbolizing the transfer of magical knowledge. Freyja's connection to seidr underscores her dual nature, encompassing both the nurturing and destructive aspects of magic. As a mistress of seidr, Freyja could influence love, fertility, and battle outcomes, reflecting her multifaceted role in Norse mythology. Her mastery of seidr emphasizes the importance of this magical practice within the divine hierarchy and its integral role in shaping the fate of gods and humans alike.

Odin and Seidr: Odin, too, is linked to seidr, despite it being traditionally associated with women. His involvement in seidr reflects his relentless quest for wisdom and mastery over all forms of magic. Odin's practice of seidr, a traditionally female art, highlights his boundary-crossing nature and his pursuit of knowledge at any cost. This pursuit led him to transcend conventional gender roles, further illustrating his complex and enigmatic character. Odin's use of seidr complements his broader repertoire of magical skills, including rune magic and shamanic practices, making him the epitome of a wise and powerful deity.

Conclusion: Seidr, as a powerful form of Norse magic, played a crucial role in the spiritual and cultural life of the Vikings. Through trance-induced rituals and communication with the spirit world, seidr practitioners could alter the course of events and access hidden knowledge. The association of seidr with both Freyja and Odin underscores its significance and complexity. Freyja's nurturing and destructive capabilities and Odin's boundary-crossing quest for wisdom exemplify the dualities within Norse mythology. The practice of seidr remains a fascinating aspect of Norse culture, highlighting the interplay between gender, magic, and the pursuit of power and knowledge.

The Völva: Norse Seeress

The völva, or seeress, was respected and powerful in Viking society. These women were skilled in seidr and divination, offering their services to predict the future and advise on important matters. As intermediaries between the mortal and divine realms, völvas were pivotal figures in the spiritual life of the Norse people.

The Role of the Völva

Völvas were often itinerant, traveling between communities and offering their prophetic abilities in exchange for hospitality and gifts. They were sought after for their insights into the future, particularly in times of crisis or uncertainty. The völva's role extended beyond mere fortune-telling; she was a spiritual guide, healer, and

154

advisor whose counsel was invaluable to leaders and common folk alike. The respect accorded to völvas reflected the Norse reverence for those who could navigate the unseen realms and provide guidance grounded in spiritual authority.

Rituals and Tools

The völva used various tools and rituals to perform their magic. Staffs inscribed with runes and symbols were common, as were ceremonial garments that denoted their status. These staffs were believed to be conduits of magical power, enhancing the völva's ability to connect with the spiritual world. Rituals often involved chanting, drumming, and the consumption of herbal concoctions to induce trance states. These practices allowed the völva to enter altered states of consciousness where she could communicate with spirits and divine the future. Specific chants and incantations, known as galdr, were essential in focusing and directing magical energies during these rituals.

Historical Accounts

In the Norse sagas, particularly the Saga of Erik the Red, völvas, or seeresses, played significant roles, though the primary focus often remained on the exploits of the Viking explorers. However, a fascinating episode involving a völva and Erik the Red offers insight into the interplay between Viking leaders and these mystical figures.

Erik the Red, known for founding the first Norse settlements in Greenland, was a legendary figure in Norse history. During his time, the völvas were highly regarded for their ability to foresee the future and offer counsel during times of uncertainty. One notable völva associated with Erik the Red's saga is Þorbjörg Lítilvölva (Thorbjorg the Little Prophetess).

155

According to the saga, during a particularly harsh winter in Greenland, the settlers faced severe famine and dwindling resources. In desperate need of guidance and hope, the community decided to consult Þorbjörg, who was renowned for her prophetic abilities. It was customary for people to seek the wisdom of völvas during crises, and Þorbjörg's reputation made her the natural choice.

Þorbjörg was invited to the home of a local chieftain named Þorkell (Thorkell), where she was treated with great respect. The völva arrived dressed in her distinctive blue cloak adorned with precious stones and a headpiece, symbolizing her sacred role. She carried a staff, which was a symbol of her power and authority as a seeress.

Erik the Red was a prominent leader among the settlers during this gathering. While the sagas do not provide explicit details about Erik's direct interaction with Þorbjörg, it is implied that he, along with the other leaders and community members, eagerly awaited her prophecy. The völva was given a seat of honor and served a special meal, including dishes made from the hearts of various animals, believed to be spiritually significant.

For her seiðr ritual, Þorbjörg requested the assistance of a woman who knew the traditional songs associated with the ritual. Guðríðr, a young woman staying with Þorkell, was chosen to sing the chants. Although Guðríðr initially hesitated due to her Christian beliefs, she eventually agreed to sing, and her voice filled the hall as Þorbjörg performed her ceremony.

After the ritual, Þorbjörg revealed her prophecy. She assured the anxious settlers that the harsh winter would soon end, and that the famine would give way to abundance. Her words brought much-needed hope and relief to the community. The prophecy's accuracy was later confirmed as the winter eased, and the settlers' situation improved.

The story of the völva and Erik the Red illustrates the crucial role that völvas played in Norse society. They were not only spiritual guides but also held considerable influence in decision-making processes, particularly during times of crisis. Although the sagas primarily highlight the exploits of Viking leaders like Erik the Red, the presence of figures like Þorbjörg demonstrates the deep cultural and spiritual traditions that intertwined with their history.

Conclusion

The völva's role in Norse society was multifaceted, blending elements of magic, spirituality, and practical counsel. As practitioners of seidr and skilled diviners, völvas were vital to the Vikings' understanding of their world and their place within it. Their rituals and tools, deeply embedded in Norse cultural practices, highlight the intricate relationship between magic and daily life. The historical accounts of völvas, such as the saga of Erik the Red, offer a glimpse into the profound influence these women wielded. The legacy of the völva endures as a testament to the enduring power and mystique of Norse magical traditions.

The Practical Magic of Everyday Life

Magic in Viking culture was not confined to grand rituals and prophecies but permeated everyday life. Charms, amulets, and spells were commonly used to protect against harm, ensure good fortune, and influence various aspects of daily existence. This everyday magic was a vital part of the Norse belief system, seamlessly integrating the supernatural into the mundane.

Protective Amulets

Amulets inscribed with runes or shaped like Thor's hammer were worn for protection and luck. These charms were believed to invoke the power of the gods to shield the wearer from danger and bring prosperity. Thor's hammer, Mjölnir, was particularly popular, symbolizing Thor's role as a protector. Other common amulets included symbols like the Valknut, which was associated with Odin and the slain warriors, and various runes known for their protective qualities. These amulets were not only personal talismans but also served as statements of faith and cultural identity.

Household Magic

Households often had protective symbols carved into doorframes or placed in strategic locations to ward off evil spirits. Everyday objects, such as tools and utensils, were sometimes marked with runes to enhance their efficacy and ensure their owner's safety. The practice of inscribing runes on household items reflects the Norse belief in the pervasive power of magic. For instance, the rune *Algiz*, symbolizing protection, might be carved into doorways or furniture to create a barrier against malevolent forces. This integration of magic into daily life underscores the Norse understanding of a world where the spiritual and physical realms were closely intertwined.

Love Spells and Fertility Rites

Magic related to love and fertility was common, reflecting the importance of family and lineage in Viking society. Spells and rituals were performed to attract a partner, ensure successful childbirth, and maintain harmony within the family. These practices were often conducted with the aid of völvas or other knowledgeable practitioners. Rituals might include the use of specific herbs, chants, and symbolic actions designed to invoke the desired outcome. Fertility rites, for example, could involve invoking the goddess Freyja, who was associated with love and fertility, to bless a union or ensure the health of a newborn. The prevalence of such magic highlights the central role of family and community in Viking life.

The practical magic of everyday life in Viking culture reveals a society deeply connected to the supernatural. Through the use of protective amulets, household magic, and love spells, the Vikings sought to harness the power of the gods and the natural world to navigate their daily challenges. This integration of magic into routine activities reflects the Norse belief in a world where the divine and the mundane were inextricably linked. The enduring legacy of these practices offers insight into the rich spiritual life of the Vikings and their pragmatic approach to magic and religion.

The Symbolism of Norse Mythology

Norse mythology is rich with symbols that carry deep meaning and reflect the beliefs and values of the Viking people. Understanding these symbols provides insight into their world's spiritual and cultural fabric. Each symbol embodies a unique aspect of Norse cosmology, offering a window into the Norse values and worldview.

Yggdrasil: The World Tree

Yggdrasil, the immense and sacred ash tree, is pivotal in Norse cosmology and mythology. It is not merely a tree but the very backbone of the universe, serving as a vital link between the nine worlds that comprise existence in Norse belief. These nine realms include Asgard (the home of the Aesir gods), Midgard (the world of humans), Jotunheim (the land of giants), Vanaheim (the realm of the Vanir gods), Alfheim (home of the light elves), Svartalfheim (realm of the dark elves or dwarves), Nidavellir (another realm of dwarves, sometimes conflated with Svartalfheim), Muspelheim (the world of fire), Niflheim (the world of ice), and Helheim (the realm of the dead). Yggdrasil's vast branches and deep roots connect these worlds, symbolizing the interconnectedness of all existence and the seamless flow between different realms of being.

The roots and branches of Yggdrasil are rich with profound symbolism, representing the cyclical nature of life, death, and rebirth, as well as the delicate balance between mortal and divine realms. Three major roots extend from Yggdrasil, each anchoring the tree into different cosmic planes. One root reaches into Asgard, the realm of the gods, and is nourished by the sacred Well of Urd. Here, the three Norns—Urd (Past), Verdandi (Present), and Skuld (Future)—tend to the well and weave the destinies of all beings, gods and mortals alike. They sprinkle the tree with water from the well to keep it alive, symbolizing the ongoing care required to maintain the fabric of existence.

Another root stretches into Jotunheim, the land of the giants, and ends at the Well of Mimir, also known as the Well of Wisdom. Mimir, a being of immense knowledge, guards this well. It was here that Odin, the All-Father and chief of the Aesir gods, sacrificed one of his eyes in exchange for a drink from the well, gaining unparalleled wisdom. This act underscores the theme of sacrifice for greater knowledge, a recurring motif in Norse mythology.

The third root extends into Niflheim or, in some accounts, directly into Helheim, the realm of the dead overseen by the goddess Hel. Near this root lies the spring Hvergelmir, where the dragon (or serpent) Nidhogg gnaws incessantly at the roots of Yggdrasil. Nidhogg represents the forces of chaos and destruction, constantly threatening the stability of the cosmos. This eternal gnawing is counteracted by the care of the Norns and other benevolent beings, illustrating the balance between creation and destruction.

High among Yggdrasil's branches resides a wise eagle, whose piercing gaze observes all that happens in the world. Between the eagle's eyes sits a hawk named Vedrfolnir. The constant exchange of insults and messages between the eagle and Nidhogg is facilitated by Ratatoskr, a mischievous squirrel who scurries up and down the trunk. Ratatoskr's actions symbolize the spread of gossip and the potential for miscommunication to sow discord—a reflection on the nature of conflict in the world.

Four stags—Dáinn, Dvalinn, Duneyrr, and Duraþrór—graze on the tree's leaves, possibly representing the four winds or seasons, contributing to the cyclical aspects of time and nature. Countless serpents also dwell beneath the tree, adding to the complex interplay of forces that influence the health of Yggdrasil and, by extension, the universe.

Often referred to as the axis mundi, or the world's axis, Yggdrasil effectively binds together the various realms of existence. Its towering branches reach into the heavens, touching the abode of the gods, while its sturdy trunk stands in Midgard, the world of humans. The tree's existence ensures the cohesion of the universe, maintaining the order and balance essential for all forms of life to continue. It serves as a cosmic meeting place where gods convene in council, highlighting its role as a central point of communication and governance.

Yggdrasil embodies the profound Norse belief in the interconnectedness of life, death, and rebirth, reflecting their understanding of the cyclical nature of the cosmos. The tree is a living entity that experiences suffering and decay, as seen in the threats posed by Nidhogg and other creatures, yet it endures through the care of the Norns and the respect of the gods. This dynamic illustrates the Norse acceptance of life's hardships alongside its beauties—a recognition that struggle and perseverance are intrinsic to existence.

During Ragnarök, the prophesied apocalypse in Norse mythology, Yggdrasil is said to tremble as the worlds face destruction. However, the tree itself survives, and from its shelter emerge Lif and Lifthrasir, two humans who will repopulate the new world. This narrative underscores themes of renewal and the eternal cycle of life, emphasizing that endings are also beginnings in the grand tapestry of existence.

163

In addition to its cosmological significance, Yggdrasil has influenced countless works of art, literature, and modern interpretations of mythology. It continues to be a powerful symbol of life, growth, and the profound connections that bind all things together. The tree reminds us of the intricate web of relationships that make up the universe and encourages a deeper appreciation for the balance and interdependence inherent in all forms of life.

Yggdrasil's enduring legacy speaks to universal themes that transcend time and culture, resonating with contemporary audiences who find meaning in its representation of unity, resilience, and the perpetual dance of creation and destruction. It serves as a timeless metaphor for the complexity of the cosmos and our place within it, inviting reflection on the unseen forces that shape our lives and the world around us.

Thor's Hammer, Mjölnir

The legendary Mjölnir, the iconic hammer wielded by Thor, was not just a formidable weapon but also a powerful symbol of protection, embodying the immense strength of Thor and his role as the defender of both the gods and humanity. Forged by the dwarven brothers Brokkr and Eitri (or Sindri, in some accounts), Mjölnir was created after a challenge from Loki, and despite a mishap during its forging—which resulted in its characteristic short handle—the hammer became the most treasured weapon among the gods.

People often wore amulets crafted in the likeness of Mjölnir as a way of seeking protection and connecting with Thor's formidable power. These amulets were especially significant during the Viking Age, serving not only as protective talismans but also as symbols of pagan faith in the face of the growing influence of Christianity. Wearing a Mjölnir amulet was a statement of cultural identity and religious belief, reinforcing one's connection to Norse traditions and the old gods.

Known for its extraordinary might, the hammer was believed to have the ability to shatter mountains. It was indispensable in safeguarding Asgard—the celestial realm of the gods—from formidable adversaries such as giants, trolls, and the serpent Jörmungandr. In numerous myths, Thor used Mjölnir to battle these chaotic forces, demonstrating his unparalleled strength and the hammer's essential role in maintaining cosmic order. The hammer had the magical property of always returning to Thor's hand after being thrown, and it could also shrink to fit inside his shirt when not in use, highlighting its mystical qualities.

As a symbol, Mjölnir epitomizes the Norse principles of protection, fortitude, and tenacity. It represents the enduring struggle between order and chaos, good and evil, and the defense of one's home and community against external threats. Additionally, it held great significance in sacred ceremonies, where it was used to bestow blessings upon marriages, births, and even funerals, showcasing its dual nature as a force that could both destroy and create. Thor's hammer was invoked to sanctify unions, bless the harvest, and protect the deceased on their journey to the afterlife, underscoring its integral role in the spiritual life of the Norse people.

Moreover, Mjölnir's influence extended beyond mythology into archaeological findings, where numerous Mjölnir pendants and carvings have been discovered across Scandinavia, attesting to its widespread veneration. Its legacy continues today, symbolizing strength, protection, and a connection to ancestral heritage. Mjölnir remains a powerful emblem in contemporary culture, appearing in literature, art, and media. It is often embraced by those who identify with Norse paganism or admire the timeless virtues it represents.

The Helm of Awe

Ægishjálmr is a symbol of protection and invincibility, often used in magic to induce fear and ensure victory in battle. It was believed to confer great power upon its wearer, making it a potent emblem of courage and dominance. Warriors would paint the Helm of Awe on their foreheads or inscribe it on their shields to gain a psychological edge over their enemies. The symbol's intricate design, often resembling a series of radial arms, was meant to project an aura of intimidation and supernatural strength. The Helm of Awe underscores the Norse warrior ethos and the importance of psychological warfare in maintaining dominance and ensuring survival.

Conclusion

The symbols of Norse mythology are more than mere decorative motifs; they are profound expressions of the Norse understanding of the universe and their place within it. From Yggdrasil's representation of interconnectedness to the Valknut's embodiment of the cycle of life and death, these symbols offer deep insights into Norse beliefs and values. Thor's hammer, Mjölnir, and the Helm of Awe highlight the importance of protection, strength, and psychological prowess in Viking culture. Together, these symbols weave a rich tapestry that illustrates the spiritual and cultural landscape of the Norse, providing timeless lessons and reflections on the human condition.

Reflect on the themes of fate, destiny, and the power of symbols, exploring how magic was both a spiritual and practical aspect of Viking life. Norse magic is a testament to the Vikings' deep connection to their gods, environment, and the unseen forces that shaped their world.

Now that we have explored the magical practices and symbols of the Norse, consider how these ancient traditions resonate with modern beliefs and practices. Reflect on the power of symbols and the enduring human desire to understand and influence the world. Let the magic of the Vikings inspire you to explore the mystical aspects of your life and appreciate the rich heritage of Norse mythology.

Chapter 6:

Modern Influence and

Interpretations

Norse Mythology in Literature

The profound and far-reaching influence of Norse mythology on modern literature is a testament to its enduring appeal and the timeless nature of its themes. For centuries, authors have drawn from the rich well of Norse legends to craft new stories, reinterpret old ones, and explore universal concepts such as heroism, fate, and the struggle between good and evil. The gods, heroes, and mythical creatures of Norse lore have provided fertile ground for creativity, sparking intrigue and eagerness among readers to delve deeper into these ancient narratives.

J.R.R. Tolkien and Middle-earth

One of the most notable influences of Norse mythology is seen in the works of J.R.R. Tolkien, whose seminal creations, *The Hobbit* and *The Lord of the Rings* trilogy, have left an indelible mark on the fantasy genre. Tolkien, a philologist and scholar of ancient languages and mythologies, infused his Middle-earth legendarium with elements drawn directly from Norse myth. The very structure of his world, with its elves, dwarves, dragons, and epic quests, echoes the sagas and eddas of Norse lore.

Characters and Races Inspired by Norse Myth

- **Elves and Dwarves**: Tolkien depicts elves as wise, immortal beings and dwarves as stout, skilled craftsmen, mirroring their portrayals in Norse mythology. The dwarves' names in *The Hobbit*, such as Thorin, Balin, and Dwalin, are taken directly from the *Dvergatal*, a section of the Poetic Edda that lists dwarf names.
- **Gandalf and Odin**: The character Gandalf resembles Odin, the All-Father of Norse mythology. Both are wise old men with long beards and wanderers with great knowledge and magical abilities. Odin is known for his quest for wisdom, even sacrificing an eye for it, paralleling Gandalf's role as a guide and mentor who often withholds information to spur others toward their destinies.

171

- **The One Ring and Andvaranaut**: The concept of a powerful ring that brings doom upon its bearer can be traced back to the Norse legend of **Andvaranaut**, a cursed ring owned by the dwarf Andvari. This ring brings misfortune to all who possess it, much like the One Ring in Tolkien's works.

Themes and Motifs

- **Fate and Destiny**: The inescapable nature of fate, a prominent theme in Norse mythology, is reflected in Tolkien's narratives. Characters like Frodo and Aragorn grapple with their destinies, much like heroes in Norse sagas who face prophesied challenges and must rise to meet them despite personal costs.
- **The Hero's Journey**: The epic quests undertaken by Tolkien's characters mirror the journeys of Norse heroes such as Sigurd, who slays the dragon Fafnir. The struggle against overwhelming odds and the personal sacrifices made by the protagonists highlight themes of courage, honor, and resilience.
- **The End of an Age**: The concept of a world-ending battle, akin to Ragnarök, is echoed in the climactic battles of Middle-earth. The passing of the old order and the rise of a new era are central to both Tolkien's work and Norse mythology, emphasizing renewal and the cyclical nature of time.

Language and Lore

- **Creation of Languages**: Tolkien's creation of Elvish languages, such as Quenya and Sindarin, was influenced by his study of Old Norse and other ancient tongues. This linguistic depth adds authenticity and richness to his world.

- **Mythical Creatures**: Creatures like trolls, wargs, and dragons in Tolkien's universe have counterparts in Norse myths, reflecting shared archetypes and storytelling traditions.

Tolkien's deep admiration for Norse mythology is evident in his meticulous world-building and character development. His ability to weave elements of these ancient myths into his narrative framework has had a lasting impact on the fantasy genre, inspiring countless authors and creators. Through Middle-earth, Tolkien has ensured that the spirit of Norse mythology continues to enchant and inspire new generations of readers.

Neil Gaiman and Modern Mythmaking

Another prominent author influenced by Norse mythology is **Neil Gaiman**, whose works often blend myth with contemporary settings to explore timeless themes and human experiences.

"American Gods"

In "American Gods," Gaiman brings the Norse gods into modern America, portraying them as deities struggling to survive in a world that has largely forgotten them. Odin, under the guise of Mr. Wednesday, is a central character who embodies the old gods' fight to remain relevant amidst the rise of new gods representing technology, media, and consumerism.

- **Themes of Identity and Belief**: The novel explores how the power of gods is linked to human belief and worship. Odin's cunning and adaptability showcase his efforts to reclaim his lost influence, reflecting the enduring nature of myth in shaping human culture.
- **Myth in the Modern World**: Gaiman's portrayal highlights the clash between ancient traditions and modern values, emphasizing that myths continue to resonate even as society evolves. The interactions between

gods and humans delve into issues of faith, purpose, and the search for meaning.

"Norse Mythology"

In his book "Norse Mythology," Gaiman retells the classic myths with a fresh perspective, making them accessible to contemporary readers.

- **Engaging Narrative Style**: Gaiman captures the humor, tragedy, and drama inherent in these ancient stories, breathing new life into tales of Thor, Loki, and other legendary figures. His storytelling emphasizes the gods' personalities, flaws, and adventures.

- **Preservation of Legacy**: By reintroducing these myths to modern audiences, Gaiman ensures that the rich legacy of Norse mythology remains alive, highlighting its relevance and appeal. His work serves as both an introduction for newcomers and a nuanced retelling for those familiar with the tales.

Impact on Modern Literature

Gaiman's works have significantly impacted modern literature, illustrating the enduring appeal of Norse mythology. His ability to intertwine mythological elements with modern storytelling offers new avenues for exploring themes of power, identity, and survival.

- **Influence on Other Media**: "American Gods" has been adapted into a television series, further expanding the reach of Norse mythology in popular culture.

- **Exploration of Universal Themes**: Gaiman's narratives often delve into the complexities of morality, destiny, and the human condition, drawing parallels between ancient myths and contemporary life.

- **Beyond Tolkien and Gaiman: The Ongoing Legacy:** Norse mythology's influence extends beyond Tolkien and Gaiman's works, permeating various facets of literature and entertainment.

Marvel Comics and the MCU

- **Thor and Loki**: Marvel Comics introduced Thor and Loki as superhero characters, reimagining the Norse gods in a modern context. The Marvel Cinematic Universe (MCU) has popularized these characters globally through blockbuster films.
- **Adaptation and Reinvention**: While taking creative liberties, these adaptations maintain core aspects of the original myths, introducing themes of family, responsibility, and identity to new audiences.

Literary Works and Retellings

- **"Runemarks" by Joanne Harris**: This novel reimagines Norse myths in a fantasy setting, exploring themes of magic, destiny, and the struggle between order and chaos.
- **"The Gospel of Loki"**: Joanne Harris also tells the Norse myths from Loki's perspective, offering a unique take on his character and motivations.
- **"The Long Dark Tea-Time of the Soul" by Douglas Adams**: Incorporating Norse gods into a humorous and satirical narrative, Adams explores their interactions with the modern world.

Themes and Relevance in Modern Literature

The continued interest in Norse mythology reflects its rich thematic content and adaptability.

Exploration of Universal Concepts

- **Heroism and Sacrifice**: Tales of bravery and self-sacrifice in Norse myths resonate with contemporary narratives, emphasizing the value of courage and integrity.

- **Fate vs. Free Will**: The tension between destiny and autonomy is a prevalent theme, prompting reflection on personal agency and the forces that shape our lives.

- **Cultural Identity**: Norse mythology often explores the relationship between individuals and their heritage, a topic relevant in today's globalized society.

Symbolism and Archetypes

- **Mythical Creatures and Symbols**: Dragons, giants, and magical artifacts from Norse myths serve as powerful symbols in literature, representing internal and external challenges.

- **Moral Complexity**: Characters like Loki embody ambiguity, allowing authors to explore the shades of gray in morality and ethics.

Conclusion

The influence of Norse mythology on literature is vast and multifaceted. Through the works of authors like J.R.R. Tolkien and Neil Gaiman, ancient myths have been reimagined and brought into new contexts, allowing them to resonate with modern audiences. These stories continue to explore universal themes, connecting the past with the present and ensuring that the rich tapestry of Norse mythology remains a vibrant and integral part of our cultural heritage.

The enduring fascination with Norse myths demonstrates their ability to adapt and remain relevant, offering insights into human nature and the complexities of existence. As literature continues to evolve, the gods, heroes, and legends of Norse mythology will undoubtedly inspire future generations of writers and readers alike, keeping the ancient narratives alive and flourishing in the collective imagination.

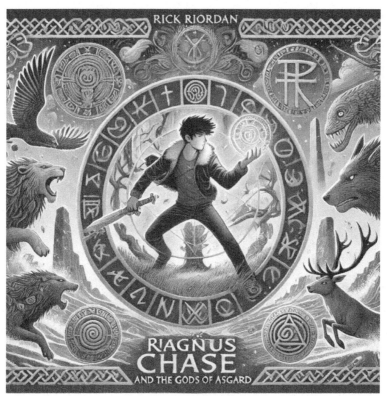

Rick Riordan's "Magnus Chase and the Gods of Asgard"

Rick Riordan's "Magnus Chase" series introduces young readers to Norse mythology through the adventures of a modern-day demigod. By weaving the myths into contemporary settings and relatable characters, Riordan educates and entertains, making the ancient stories accessible and engaging for younger audiences.

The series follows Magnus Chase, a teenager who discovers he is the son of a Norse god. Through his journey, readers encounter a rich tapestry of Norse deities, mythical creatures, and legendary heroes, all reimagined in a modern context. Riordan's storytelling blends humor, action, and mythological lore, offering a fresh take on the ancient tales while staying true to their essence.

Riordan's skillful adaptation of Norse mythology for a younger audience ensures that these timeless stories continue to be passed down, instilling a sense of wonder and curiosity about ancient cultures. The "Magnus Chase" series not only entertains but also serves as a gateway for young readers to explore the rich world of Norse myths, fostering a deeper appreciation for history and literature.

Norse Mythology in Film and Television

The Marvel Cinematic Universe (MCU) has undeniably left a profound mark on the contemporary perception of Norse mythology. Iconic figures such as Thor, Loki, and Odin have transcended into common parlance, courtesy of their portrayals in blockbuster movies. While these adaptations may take creative liberties, they kindle a fascination with the original myths and underscore the timeless allure of these age-old characters.

Chris Hemsworth's depiction of Thor skillfully intertwines traits of the mythological hero with contemporary superhero characteristics, seamlessly blending ancient and modern narratives. Tom Hiddleston's portrayal of Loki adeptly captures the enigmatic charm and intricate nature of the trickster, adding to a revitalized captivation with Norse legends. The MCU's vivid portrayal of Asgard and its inhabitants brings the mythic realm to a vast, global audience, rendering the ancient tales accessible to new generations.

Vikings (TV Series)

The History Channel's "Vikings" series delves into the lives of legendary Viking heroes like Ragnar Lothbrok. The show combines historical events with mythological elements, exploring the beliefs and practices of the Viking Age. Through its narrative, "Vikings" offers a glimpse into how Norse mythology influenced the daily lives, decisions, and worldview of the Norse people.

"Vikings" meticulously portrays the culture and society of the Norse, blending historical accuracy with mythological intrigue. Characters frequently interact with the divine, having visions of gods like Odin and interpreting omens that guide their actions. These elements reflect the deep-seated belief in fate (wyrd) and the omnipresence of the gods in the Vikings' understanding of the world.

The series also highlights key aspects of Norse mythology and religious practices, such as seidr magic, sacred rituals, and sacrifices. By showcasing these traditions, "Vikings" not only entertains but also educates viewers about the spiritual and cultural landscape of the Norse people. Through the epic tales of Ragnar, Lagertha, and their descendants, "Vikings" brings to life the enduring power and relevance of Norse myths, illustrating their impact on the collective psyche and daily practices of the Viking Age.

The Last Kingdom: Based on Bernard Cornwell's "The Saxon Stories," the "Last Kingdom" series features Norse and Saxon characters, highlighting their cultural and mythological clashes. The portrayal of Norse gods and rituals provides insight into the spiritual landscape of the time, blending historical fiction with mythological themes.

"The Last Kingdom" follows the journey of Uhtred of Bebbanburg, a Saxon nobleman raised by Vikings, as he navigates the turbulent world of 9th—and 10th-century England. The series vividly depicts the conflict and coexistence between Norse paganism and emerging Christianity, reflecting the complex cultural dynamics of the era. Through Uhtred's dual identity, viewers experience the stark contrasts and subtle similarities between the Norse and Saxon worlds.

Norse mythology is intricately woven into the narrative, showcasing rituals, sacrifices, and beliefs that shape the characters' actions and destinies. The series portrays the reverence for gods like Odin and Thor and the significance of symbols such as runes and amulets. These elements highlight the Norse understanding of fate, honor, and the supernatural, providing a rich backdrop for the characters' struggles and triumphs.

"The Last Kingdom" brings historical events to life and delves into the mythological and spiritual underpinnings that influenced them. By blending historical fiction with mythological themes, the series offers a nuanced portrayal of the era, illuminating the profound impact of Norse mythology on the lives and beliefs of its characters.

Norse Mythology in Music and Art

Music and art have long drawn inspiration from Norse mythology, using its themes and characters to explore complex emotions and ideas.

Richard Wagner's "Der Ring des Nibelungen": This stands as one of the most ambitious and influential works in the operatic canon, spanning four epic operas: "Das Rheingold," "Die Walküre," "Siegfried," and "Götterdämmerung." Composed over 26 years, this monumental cycle draws heavily from Norse mythology and the medieval German epic, the Nibelungenlied, to weave a complex narrative of gods, heroes, and mythical creatures.

Das Rheingold: The cycle begins with "Das Rheingold," setting the stage for the epic saga. The opera introduces the cursed ring forged by the dwarf Alberich from the gold of the Rhine River. The ring grants immense power but brings doom to its possessor. Wotan, the chief of the gods, steals the ring to pay for the construction of Valhalla, the gods' magnificent new hall. This act of theft and betrayal sets off a chain of events that reverberates throughout the entire cycle. Themes of greed, power, and the corrupting influence of the ring are established, echoing the darker aspects of Norse mythology.

Die Walküre: In "Die Walküre," the narrative focuses on the tragic love story of the twins Siegmund and Sieglinde, children of Wotan. Their illicit love and Siegmund's death at the hands of Hunding, Sieglinde's husband, drive the plot. Brünnhilde, one of the Valkyries and Wotan's daughters, is central to this opera, and she defies her father to protect Siegmund. Her disobedience leads to her punishment—being cast into a deep sleep surrounded by a ring of fire, awaiting a hero to awaken her. The themes of love, loyalty, and rebellion against divine authority are explored with profound emotional depth, reflecting the moral complexities found in Norse sagas.

Siegfried: This follows the hero Siegfried, the son of Siegmund and Sieglinde, raised by the dwarf Mime. Unaware of his true heritage, Siegfried forges the sword Nothung, slays the dragon Fafnir, and claims the cursed ring. His fearless nature and innocence set him apart from the other characters, making him a symbol of untainted heroism. Siegfried's journey to awakening Brünnhilde with a kiss brings themes of awakening, self-discovery, and the hero's journey to the forefront. This opera delves into the hero archetype, highlighting bravery, resilience, and the inevitable encounter with destiny.

Götterdämmerung: The cycle concludes with "Götterdämmerung," or "Twilight of the Gods," depicting the ultimate downfall of the gods. Siegfried is betrayed and murdered, and Brünnhilde, overwhelmed with grief, sacrifices herself, returning the ring to the Rhine and ending its curse. The gods, having failed to uphold justice and integrity, face their destruction in the final cataclysm of Ragnarok. This opera encapsulates themes of betrayal, sacrifice, and the cyclical nature of destruction and renewal, mirroring the apocalyptic visions of Norse mythology.

Wagner's Influence and Legacy

Wagner's "Der Ring des Nibelungen" revolutionized the structure and scale of opera and brought Norse mythology to the forefront of Western culture. His use of leitmotifs—recurring musical themes associated with characters and ideas—created a richly layered narrative that deepened the characters' psychological complexity and motivations.

Through Wagner's operas, the dramatic and often tragic elements of Norse myths are brought to life with unparalleled intensity. The operatic

183

cycle remains a testament to the enduring power of these ancient stories, showcasing their relevance and impact on modern storytelling and artistic expression. Wagner's synthesis of myth, music, and drama continues to captivate audiences, ensuring that the themes and tales of Norse mythology remain vibrant and influential in contemporary culture.

Modern Metal Bands

The genre of metal music, particularly the Viking and black metal subgenres, has found profound inspiration in Norse mythology. Bands like Amon Amarth, Bathory, and Enslaved infuse their music with mythological themes, celebrating the heroic and epic nature of the ancient sagas. Their work often evokes these myths' raw power and grandeur, creating a deep connection between modern audiences and ancient tales through intense and evocative soundscapes.

Amon Amarth

A Swedish melodic death metal band stands out for their dedication to Norse themes. Named after a location from J.R.R. Tolkien's Middle-earth, the band's lyrics and imagery are steeped in Viking history and mythology. Songs like "Twilight of the Thunder God" and "Pursuit of Vikings" tell tales of gods, battles, and seafaring warriors, often drawing directly from Norse mythological sources. Their music is not just an homage to the stories but an exploration of the Viking spirit, blending aggressive rhythms with melodic elements to capture the epic and heroic nature of the sagas.

Bathory

One of the pioneers of black metal also played a crucial role in developing Viking metal. The Swedish band, named after the infamous Hungarian countess, shifted their lyrical focus in the late 1980s to Norse mythology and Viking themes. Albums like "Hammerheart" and "Twilight of the Gods" are seminal works in the Viking metal genre. Bathory's music combines raw black metal elements with epic, atmospheric compositions that evoke the grandeur of the Viking age, exploring themes of paganism, honor, and the gods of old.

Enslaved

Norwegian band Enslaved blends black metal with progressive elements, drawing heavily on Norse mythology and history. Their name itself reflects the Viking ethos of exploration and conquest. Albums such as "Frost" and "Eld" delve into the rich tapestry of Norse mythology, with lyrics that often reference ancient gods, cosmic battles, and esoteric knowledge. Enslaved's complex compositions and lyrical depth profoundly explore the mythological themes, making their music both a tribute to and an extension of Norse cultural heritage.

The Connection Between Metal and Myth

These bands, among others, bridge the gap between ancient myth and modern music, using the intensity of metal to convey the power and emotion of Norse sagas. Metal music's aggressive and grandiose nature lends itself perfectly to the epic tales of gods, warriors, and cosmic battles. By incorporating mythological themes into their lyrics and imagery, these bands pay homage to their cultural roots and keep the myths alive for contemporary audiences. Their music serves as a modern retelling of the ancient stories, ensuring that the legacy of Norse mythology continues to resonate through powerful and evocative soundscapes.

Contemporary Art: Modern artists continue to find inspiration in Norse mythology, creating works that reinterpret ancient themes for contemporary viewers. Illustrators and painters depict scenes from the sagas with new artistic techniques, while sculptors and installation artists explore the symbolic and cultural significance of Norse myths. These artworks bridge the gap between past and present, allowing audiences to engage with the myths in fresh and imaginative ways.

Norse Mythology in Video Games

Video games have become a powerful medium for storytelling, allowing players to immerse themselves in rich narratives and expansive worlds. Norse mythology, with its epic tales of gods, heroes, and mythical creatures, has found a prominent place in this interactive art form. By incorporating elements of Norse legends, game developers have created engaging experiences that both entertain and educate players about this ancient mythology.

God of War Series

One of the most notable examples of Norse mythology in video games is the "God of War" series, particularly the 2018 installment developed by Santa Monica Studio. This game marks a significant shift from the previous Greek mythology setting to the Norse world, bringing the mythology to life with stunning visuals, intricate storytelling, and deep character development.

Immersive Storytelling and Characters

187

Players step into the role of Kratos, a former Spartan god seeking redemption and a new life after the tragedies of his past. Now living in the Norse realm, he is accompanied by his young son Atreus. Their journey begins with a simple task—to fulfill the last wish of Atreus's mother by spreading her ashes from the highest peak in the Nine Realms. This quest unfolds into a complex narrative intertwining familial bonds, personal growth, and the impending threats from gods and monsters of Norse legend.

Throughout the game, players interact with prominent Norse deities such as:

Baldur is Odin and Freyja's invulnerable son, who becomes one of the main antagonists.

Freyja: A powerful goddess associated with love, fertility, and magic who aids Kratos and Atreus but harbors her own secrets.

Mimir: The wise advisor who provides lore and insight into the Norse world, accompanying the duo as a talking head.

The portrayal of these gods offers a nuanced interpretation of Norse mythology, presenting them as multifaceted characters with personal motivations and flaws.

Richly Detailed World Inspired by Norse Legends

The game's setting encompasses various realms from Norse cosmology, including:

Midgard: The mortal realm where humans reside, filled with forests, mountains, and ancient ruins.

Alfheim: The realm of the Light Elves, characterized by ethereal landscapes and mystical architecture.

Jötunheim: The land of the giants, shrouded in mystery and central to the game's overarching plot.

Players encounter mythical creatures such as:

Dragons: Majestic and fearsome beings that pose significant challenges.

Trolls and Ogres: Massive foes that test the player's combat skills.

Valkyries: Warrior maidens serving Odin are presented as formidable optional bosses guarding hidden lore.

The attention to detail in environmental design, creature aesthetics, and cultural artifacts immerses players in a world that feels authentic to Norse mythology.

Blend of Action and Narrative Depth

"God of War" masterfully combines intense action gameplay with deep narrative elements. Combat is visceral and strategic, utilizing Kratos's new weapon, the Leviathan Axe, which can be imbued with elemental magic and recalls the mythological weaponry of Norse heroes. Atreus supports his father with archery and magical abilities, reflecting his growing proficiency and confidence.

The story delves into themes such as:

Parenthood and Legacy: Kratos's relationship with Atreus explores the challenges of fatherhood, mentorship, and the desire to break the cycle of violence from his past.

Fate and Destiny: The characters grapple with prophecies and the roles they are expected to play in the impending events, echoing the Norse emphasis on fate.

Identity and Self-Discovery: Both Kratos and Atreus confront their true natures and the implications of their heritage.

The game's narrative encourages players to reflect on these themes, enriching the overall experience beyond mere action.

Educational Aspects

While primarily an entertainment medium, "God of War" also serves an educational purpose by introducing players to Norse mythology in an accessible manner. The game incorporates:

Lore Codex: An in-game encyclopedia that provides detailed information on characters, creatures, and myths encountered, written from Atreus's perspective.

Runes and Language: Authentic use of Norse runes and references to the Old Norse language enhance immersion and authenticity.

Mythological Accuracy with Creative Liberties: While the game allows for creative freedom, it remains respectful of the source material, sparking interest in the original myths.

Other Notable Games Featuring Norse Mythology

Hellblade: Senua's Sacrifice

Developed by Ninja Theory, this action-adventure game follows Senua, a Celtic warrior journeying into Helheim to save her lover's soul. The game intertwines Norse mythology with psychological horror, providing a visceral exploration of mental illness and personal demons. Players face gods and creatures like Hela, the goddess of death, and navigate environments inspired by Norse cosmology.

Assassin's Creed Valhalla

Part of Ubisoft's acclaimed series, "Assassin's Creed Valhalla" allows players to experience the Viking Age as Eivor, a Norse raider settling in England. The game seamlessly blends historical fiction with Norse mythology, featuring:

Mythical Quests: Visionary sequences where players visit Asgard and Jötunheim, interacting with gods like Odin and Thor.

Mythological Weapons and Artifacts: Discovering legendary items such as Mjölnir and Gungnir.

Cultural Representation: Showcasing Viking society, rituals, and beliefs, offering insights into their integration of mythology into daily life.

Jotun

An indie game by Thunder Lotus Games, "Jotun" is a hand-drawn action-exploration game where players control Thora, a Viking warrior seeking to impress the gods after an inglorious death. She must defeat the Jotun, elemental giants from Norse myths, to gain entrance to Valhalla. The game emphasizes exploration and features narration in Icelandic, enhancing its cultural authenticity.

The Banner Saga Series

Developed by Stoic Studio, this tactical role-playing game series is heavily influenced by Norse mythology and art. Players lead a caravan through a world inspired by Viking legend, facing moral choices and strategic battles. Themes include:

Ragnarök-like Cataclysm: An impending darkness threatens the world, mirroring the apocalyptic prophecies of Norse lore.

Mythical Creatures: Encounters with beings resembling giants and other mythical entities.

Art Style: Visuals inspired by traditional Norse art and animation, creating a unique aesthetic.

Impact and Significance

191

Cultural Education

These games introduce players to Norse mythology, sparking interest in the myths and encouraging further exploration. By engaging interactively, players gain a deeper understanding of:

Mythological Characters: Personalities, motivations, and relationships of gods like Odin, Thor, and Loki.

Mythical Creatures and Realms: Familiarity with beings like the World Serpent Jörmungandr and locations such as Helheim.

Cultural Practices: Insights into Viking rituals, values, and societal structures.

Artistic Influence

The incorporation of Norse mythology has influenced game design in:

Narrative Complexity: Utilizing rich source material to craft intricate stories with emotional depth.

Visual Design: Inspired by Norse art, symbolism, and architecture, creating immersive environments.

Music and Soundscapes: Compositions that reflect Norse musical traditions and atmospheric sound design.

Player Engagement and Community

The popularity of these games has fostered active communities where players:

Discuss and Analyze: Engaging in discussions about mythological references and interpretations.

Create Fan Works: Producing art, fiction, and other creative expressions inspired by the games.

Participate in Cultural Exchange: Sharing knowledge and resources about Norse mythology, promoting cross-cultural understanding.

Conclusion

Norse mythology's integration into video games demonstrates the medium's capacity to bring ancient stories to life in innovative and interactive ways. Through engaging gameplay, compelling narratives, and authentic representations, games like "God of War" and others offer players both entertainment and education. They provide a gateway to the rich tapestry of Norse myths, allowing players to experience and participate in these timeless tales.

This fusion of mythology and modern technology preserves these ancient stories and revitalizes them, ensuring their relevance for contemporary audiences. By exploring themes of heroism, fate, and the human condition, these games resonate with players on a profound level, reflecting the enduring power of Norse mythology in shaping art and culture.

Chapter 7:

Reflecting on the Journey

Reflecting on the Timelessness of Norse Mythology

As we near the end of our journey, reflect on the timelessness of Norse mythology and its profound impact on human imagination and culture. These myths, woven with themes of heroism, fate, and the struggle between order and chaos, continue to resonate with us today. By examining the stories of gods, giants, and heroes, we gain a deeper understanding of the values and beliefs that shaped Viking society and continue to influence modern thought.

The Enduring Appeal of Norse Myths

Norse mythology has captivated audiences for centuries; its stories are filled with powerful deities, epic battles, and profound wisdom. The allure of these myths lies in their ability to speak to the human experience, exploring themes that are as relevant today as they were in the Viking Age.

These myths offer a rich tapestry of narratives that delve into human nature's complexities, fate's inevitability, and the perennial struggle between order and chaos. The gods, giants, and heroes of Norse mythology are not just fantastical beings but also reflections of the virtues, vices, and emotions that define humanity. Through their stories, we can explore themes of bravery, sacrifice, love, and revenge, gaining insights into our lives and the world around us.

Moreover, Norse mythology's profound impact on modern culture underscores its timeless relevance. From literature and film to music and art, these ancient tales inspire and resonate, demonstrating their enduring power to captivate and influence. By studying these myths, we preserve the Viking Age's rich heritage and find timeless lessons and inspiration that remain pertinent in our contemporary world.

The Nature of Heroism

The tales of Odin, Thor, Sigurd, and Beowulf exemplify the Norse concept of heroism. These heroes confront insurmountable odds with bravery and determination, embodying the virtues of courage, honor, and resilience. Their legendary deeds are not merely about physical might but also the inner strength required to uphold one's principles in the face of adversity.

Odin's relentless quest for wisdom, even at the cost of his own eye, symbolizes the pursuit of knowledge and the sacrifice it often entails. Thor's unyielding courage as he battles the giants and defends Asgard demonstrates a true hero's protective and persevering nature. Sigurd's slaying of the dragon Fafnir and his tragic love story with Brynhild highlight the themes of fate and the personal cost of heroism. Beowulf's battles against Grendel, Grendel's mother, and the dragon illustrate the hero's journey and the ultimate sacrifice for the greater good.

Their stories inspire us to face our challenges with similar courage, reminding us that heroism is about more than physical strength—it is about the strength of character. The enduring appeal of these heroes lies in their ability to embody the qualities we admire and aspire to, encouraging us to confront our fears, uphold our values, and persevere through life's trials with honor and resilience.

The Role of Fate

Fate, or wyrd, plays a central role in Norse mythology, shaping the destinies of gods and mortals. This concept underscores the belief that the course of events in the universe is predetermined by a complex web of cause and effect woven by the Norns—three mythical beings who spin the threads of fate. In Norse lore, even the mightiest gods are subject to the immutable decrees of fate, highlighting the omnipotence of this force.

The acceptance of fate, coupled with the courage to meet it head-on, reflects a worldview that values both individual agency and the larger cosmic order. Heroes and gods alike confront their destinies with a sense of duty and bravery, knowing their actions are part of a grander scheme. Odin, for instance, willingly sacrifices his eye to gain wisdom about the runes, fully aware that his knowledge will ultimately contribute to the unfolding of Ragnarok, the end of the world.

This duality encourages us to recognize our own agency while understanding that we are part of a greater whole. It teaches that while we can exert influence over our lives, we must also accept the inherent unpredictability of existence. By embracing this balance, we learn to navigate life's challenges with a more profound sense of purpose and resilience, acknowledging that our paths are intertwined with the broader tapestry of the universe.

The Balance of Order and Chaos

The constant struggle between order and chaos is a recurring theme in Norse mythology. This dynamic is embodied by characters like Loki, whose mischief often disrupts the balance of the cosmos, and Thor, whose battles against giants and monsters aim to restore it. Loki's unpredictable nature and penchant for causing trouble are catalysts for many myths, setting events that challenge the established order. His actions, whether driven by malice or curiosity, force the gods to confront and adapt to the ensuing chaos.

Thor, conversely, symbolizes the force of order and protection. His relentless combat against the chaotic elements, represented by the giants and other malevolent beings, underscores his role as a guardian of the divine realm. The thunder god's strength and determination to uphold stability make him crucial in maintaining the cosmic balance.

Ragnarok's ultimate conflict illustrates the delicate balance between these forces on a grand scale. Ragnarok, the prophesied end of the world, is a cataclysmic event where order and chaos clash in a final, devastating battle. This apocalypse is a narrative of destruction and a cycle of renewal, where the old world perishes to give way to a new one. It emphasizes that chaos, while destructive, is also a necessary force for transformation and rebirth.

This theme resonates with the human condition, highlighting the need to navigate life's complexities and maintain harmony in the face of chaos. Just as the gods struggle to balance order and chaos, individuals must find their equilibrium amid the uncertainties and challenges of life. The myths of Norse mythology remind us that chaos is an integral part of existence, and our ability to confront and integrate it into our lives defines our strength and resilience.

Embracing the Lessons of Norse Mythology

As we have explored throughout this book, Norse mythology offers a rich tapestry of stories and lessons that continue to inspire and educate. The myths provide a lens through which we can view the world, offering insights into human nature, societal values, and the timeless struggle between light and dark, good and evil. These ancient tales, woven with themes of heroism, fate, and the balance between order and chaos, resonate deeply with the human experience, reminding us of the enduring power of myth.

Norse mythology invites us to reflect on our own lives, find courage in the face of adversity, and appreciate all things' interconnectedness. The stories of gods and heroes, with their trials and triumphs, mirror our own challenges and aspirations. Whether it is Odin's relentless pursuit of wisdom, Thor's unyielding protection of his realm, or Loki's complex dance between creation and destruction, these characters embody the virtues and vices that define humanity.

Whether you are a scholar, a casual reader, or someone seeking to understand the deeper meanings behind these ancient tales, Norse mythology has something to offer. It teaches us the importance of bravery, honor, and resilience and the necessity of embracing the light and shadows within ourselves. By engaging with these myths, we preserve the Viking Age's cultural heritage and enrich our understanding of life's complexities and the universal quest for meaning.

Cultural and Historical Impact

Norse mythology is a collection of stories that reflect the Viking way of life. The myths provided a framework for understanding the world, influencing everything from legal practices to daily rituals.

198

Societal Norms and Values

The values embodied in Norse myths—honor, loyalty, and bravery—were integral to Viking society. These stories reinforced societal norms and guided personal behavior, creating a cohesive cultural identity. Heroes like Sigurd, with his unwavering courage, and deities like Thor, with his protective strength, set powerful examples for the Vikings to emulate. Acts of bravery in battle, loyalty to one's kin, and the pursuit of honor were not just ideals but expectations for how individuals should live.

The mythological narratives served as both moral lessons and societal guidelines. For instance, the tale of Sigurd's loyalty and heroism in slaying the dragon Fafnir underscored the importance of courage and integrity. Similarly, the sagas depicting the binding oaths and feuds among gods and mortals highlighted the critical nature of trust and honor in maintaining societal harmony.

By examining these myths, we gain insight into the social fabric of the Viking Age and the principles that governed their lives. The stories provided a common cultural touchstone that helped to unify the Norse people, ensuring that the values of their ancestors continued to shape their world. This cohesive cultural identity, rooted in mythological traditions, fostered a sense of community and continuity essential for the Vikings' survival and success in a challenging world.

Historical Legacy

The historical impact of Norse mythology extends beyond the Viking Age. As Norse explorers, traders, and settlers ventured across Europe and beyond, they carried their stories, beliefs, and cultural practices, leaving a lasting imprint on the regions they touched. These myths did not remain confined to the Scandinavian homeland; instead, they influenced a broad spectrum of European cultures, significantly shaping the historical and cultural landscape.

Place names across Europe bear witness to the legacy of Norse mythology. From the British Isles to Iceland and the coasts of France, many locations are named after Norse gods and heroes, reflecting the deep cultural integration of Norse settlers. Names like Thorshavn (Thor's harbor) and Odense (Odin's sanctuary) are enduring reminders of the Norse presence and the stories that came with them.

The influence of Norse mythology is also evident in language. Many words and expressions in modern English and other European languages have roots in Old Norse, the language of the Vikings. Terms related to seafaring, law, and daily life reveal the extent to which Norse culture permeated the societies they interacted with. For example, the English days of the week—Tuesday (Tiw's day), Wednesday (Woden's day), Thursday (Thor's day), and Friday (Frigg's day)—are derived from Norse gods, showcasing the mythology's integration into daily life.

Cultural practices, too, reflect the enduring legacy of Norse myths. Festivals, rituals, and traditions rooted in Viking customs continue to be celebrated in various forms, preserving the essence of Norse mythology. The fascination with Viking heritage and the resurgence of interest in their myths in literature, film, and popular culture underscores these ancient stories' timeless appeal and relevance.

Modern Relevance and Inspiration

The relevance of Norse mythology in contemporary culture cannot be overstated. These ancient stories continue to inspire and inform modern literature, film, art, and even scientific exploration. The timeless themes and vivid characters of Norse myths have found new life in various forms of

200

media, resonating with audiences worldwide and influencing a broad range of creative and intellectual endeavors.

Literature and Film

The continued adaptation of Norse myths in literature and film underscores their timelessness and universal appeal. These stories resonate because they explore fundamental human experiences—heroism, fate, and the struggle between order and chaos. By reimagining these myths, modern creators honor their ancient origins and keep them alive and relevant for new generations. This dynamic interplay between the old and the new ensures that Norse mythology remains a vibrant and influential part of our cultural landscape.

Scientific Exploration

The fascination with Norse mythology has also influenced scientific inquiry. Studies of Viking history and archaeology are often intertwined with exploring their myths, leading to discoveries about their culture and worldview. This intersection of myth and science enriches our understanding of both.

Archaeological Discoveries

Archaeological research has uncovered numerous artifacts that provide insight into the lives and beliefs of the Vikings. For instance, burial sites with grave goods, such as weapons, jewelry, and tools, align with mythological descriptions of the afterlife. These findings help validate the stories told in the sagas and eddas, offering tangible evidence of how mythology influenced Viking practices. The Oseberg Ship, a well-preserved Viking ship burial, is a prime example of how archaeological discoveries can illuminate the connection between myth and reality. Such sites often contain symbols and items referenced in myths, confirming their cultural significance and providing a deeper understanding of Viking life.

Historical Studies

Historians studying the Viking Age frequently draw on Norse mythology to interpret historical events and societal structures. The sagas, while sometimes mythologized, offer valuable insights into the social norms, legal practices, and daily life of the Norse people. Researchers can piece together a more comprehensive picture of the Viking world by analyzing these texts alongside historical records and archaeological findings. For example, the Icelandic sagas not only tell heroic tales but also document the legal disputes and social customs of the time, highlighting the interplay between myth and historical fact.

Linguistic Research

Linguistic studies also benefit from the exploration of Norse mythology. The Old Norse language, preserved in mythological texts, provides a rich source for understanding the linguistic development of Scandinavian languages. Researchers study the poetic and prose eddas to trace linguistic evolution, uncovering how language and mythology influenced each other. This research helps linguists reconstruct the phonetics, grammar, and vocabulary of Old Norse, contributing to our knowledge of historical linguistics.

Astronomy and Cosmology

Norse mythology's detailed cosmology, including the concept of Yggdrasil and the nine worlds, has intrigued astronomers and cosmologists. Scholars have examined how the Norse understood the universe, drawing parallels between mythological descriptions and astronomical phenomena.

202

This exploration shows how ancient cultures perceived their place in the cosmos and the natural world. The alignment of certain mythological events with celestial occurrences, such as solar and lunar eclipses, suggests that the Vikings had a sophisticated understanding of astronomy, which was deeply interwoven with their mythological narratives.

The Intersection of Myth and Science

The intersection of Norse mythology and scientific exploration highlights the enduring relevance of these ancient stories. By studying myths through the lens of science, researchers gain a holistic understanding of the Viking world, blending the mystical with the empirical. This interdisciplinary approach enriches our knowledge of Norse culture and demonstrates the universal human drive to make sense of the world through storytelling and scientific inquiry. The fusion of myth and science underscores the profound impact of Norse mythology on our understanding of history, culture, and the natural world.

Personal Reflection

On a personal level, Norse mythology invites us to reflect on our own lives and values. The themes of heroism, fate, and the struggle for balance are universal, encouraging us to consider how we navigate these aspects in our own experiences. Engaging with these ancient stories connects us with the timeless human quest for meaning and understanding.

Embracing Heroism

The stories of Odin, Thor, Sigurd, and other Norse heroes inspire us to embrace our inner strength and face challenges with courage and resilience. Heroism in Norse mythology is not merely about physical prowess but integrity, loyalty, and perseverance. These tales encourage us to stand firm in our convictions, support our loved ones, and confront our fears, reminding us that true heroism is rooted in character and action.

Understanding Fate

The concept of fate, or wyrd, plays a central role in Norse mythology, reminding us of the interplay between destiny and free will. The Norse acceptance of fate and the courage to face it head-on teaches us to recognize and respect the forces beyond our control while still striving to shape our paths. This duality encourages us to find a balance between acceptance and action, understanding that while we cannot control everything, we have the power to influence our destinies.

Balancing Order and Chaos

The perpetual struggle between order and chaos in Norse myths reflects the complexities of our own lives. Loki's mischief, Thor's battles, and the ultimate conflict of Ragnarok illustrate the need to navigate life's uncertainties and maintain harmony amidst turmoil. These stories resonate with our experiences, highlighting the importance of resilience and adaptability in facing life's challenges. They teach us to find equilibrium, embracing both the predictable and the unpredictable aspects of our journey.

Connecting with Ancient Wisdom

Engaging with Norse mythology allows us to tap into the wisdom of the past, providing insights that are still relevant today. These myths offer a lens through which we can explore our own values and beliefs, encouraging introspection and personal growth. By reflecting on the themes of heroism, fate, and balance, we gain a deeper understanding of ourselves and our place in the world.

The Timeless Quest for Meaning

Norse mythology vividly captures the timeless human quest for meaning. These stories remind us that, across time and cultures, people have sought to understand their existence, grapple with their destiny, and find their place in the cosmos. Engaging with these ancient tales connects us with a shared human heritage, finding solace and inspiration in the enduring narratives that have shaped our understanding of life and the universe.

Before progressing to the subsequent chapter, I encourage you to take a moment to deeply contemplate the captivating stories and profound lessons of Norse mythology. Ponder how the overarching themes of heroism, fate, and the delicate equilibrium between order and chaos may reverberate within the intricate tapestry of your own life. Allow the ancient narratives to ignite a spark within you, motivating you to wholeheartedly embrace your inner hero, fearlessly confront the trajectory of your destiny, and seek equilibrium amid the intricacies of existence. By exploring Norse mythology, you can unearth timeless wisdom that has transcended generations, providing invaluable guidance and enrichment to the human journey.

Conclusion

Norse mythology offers us far more than a collection of ancient stories—it provides a wealth of timeless lessons that resonate profoundly with our modern lives. The epic sagas of gods, heroes, and giants from Viking lore are not merely distant relics of the past but vivid reflections of the human condition and its ongoing struggles. These tales have traversed the ages, carrying with them themes that are as relevant today as they were in the time of the Vikings, speaking to the core of our shared humanity.

The Timeless Relevance of Norse Myths

The themes of heroism, fate, and the delicate balance between order and chaos are woven intricately into the fabric of Norse mythology. Heroes like Sigurd and Beowulf confront formidable challenges, battling external monsters and internal conflicts, symbolizing the universal human journey toward self-discovery and fulfillment. The gods themselves, such as Odin and Thor, embody virtues and flaws that mirror our own, making their stories enduringly relatable.

The concept of fate, or wyrd, plays a central role in these myths, highlighting the Norse belief in an inescapable destiny that even the gods cannot avoid. Accepting fate does not breed passivity but inspires individuals to face their destinies with courage and dignity. In a modern context, this perspective encourages us to acknowledge the aspects of life beyond our control while empowering us to act honorably and purposefully within the paths we tread.

Reflections on Modern Life

Engaging with these myths allows us to delve into the heart of Viking culture, where values such as bravery, honor, loyalty, and accepting one's destiny were central to their worldview. These stories challenge us to consider what living a life of integrity and purpose means. They remind us that the struggles we face—personal, societal, or global—are part of a larger narrative of growth and transformation.

In our fast-paced, often chaotic modern world, the Norse myths offer a unique lens through which we can draw personal inspiration. The relentless determination of characters like Thor, who battles against overwhelming odds to protect both gods and humans, inspires us to persevere in adversity.

The wisdom-seeking journey of Odin, who sacrifices greatly in his quest for knowledge, encourages us to value learning and self-improvement.

Igniting Creativity and Intellectual Pursuits

These stories can ignite our creativity, providing a wellspring of imagery, symbolism, and narrative power that fuels our own artistic and intellectual pursuits. Writers, artists, and thinkers continue to draw upon Norse mythology to explore complex themes, create compelling works, and engage audiences with the profound questions that these myths raise. The rich symbolism found in elements like Yggdrasil, the World Tree, or the runes discovered by Odin, offers deep metaphors for interconnectedness, growth, and the pursuit of wisdom.

By tapping into this mythological heritage, we can find inspiration to innovate and express ourselves in new ways. The archetypal characters and epic narratives serve as templates for storytelling, allowing us to explore contemporary issues through the lens of ancient wisdom. Whether in literature, visual arts, or other creative fields, the influence of Norse mythology continues to resonate, highlighting its enduring relevance.

Lessons in Resilience and Acceptance

As we navigate the challenges of contemporary life—uncertainty, change, and the quest for meaning—the wisdom embedded in these tales guides us in facing life's obstacles with courage and resilience. The Norse myths do not shy away from depicting hardship and loss; instead, they embrace these realities as integral parts of existence. The prophecy of Ragnarök, the world's end, illustrates a profound understanding of cycles of destruction and renewal. Even in the face of inevitable demise, the gods and heroes stand firm, exemplifying steadfastness and the belief that honor lies in how one meets one's fate.

This teaches us the value of perseverance and the importance of upholding our principles, even when outcomes are uncertain. It encourages us to find strength in adversity and view challenges as growth opportunities. The Norse emphasis on embracing one's destiny while striving to live honorably provides a framework for approaching life's unpredictability with grace and determination.

Embracing Destiny and Seeking Harmony

Embrace your destiny not as something to be feared but as a path to fulfillment. The Norse myths encourage us to balance acceptance and action, acknowledging the forces beyond our control while actively shaping our responses. By seeking harmony in existence's often chaotic and unpredictable nature, we align ourselves with a deeper understanding of the world's complexities.

The character of Loki, the trickster god, embodies the unpredictable elements of life that can disrupt order and challenge our perceptions. His actions, while often causing turmoil, also lead to growth and transformation. This duality reminds us that change, even when unsettling, is essential to the human experience. We can navigate uncertainty with greater confidence and wisdom by embracing this perspective.

Continuing the Legacy

These ancient myths are not static or confined to the past; they inspire and guide us on our modern journey. Through literature, art, film, and interactive media like video games, Norse mythology remains a vibrant part of contemporary culture. Its stories offer insights that are as relevant today as they were centuries ago, bridging the gap between past and present.

By engaging with Norse mythology, we become part of a continuum, connecting with the experiences and wisdom of those who came before us.

We carry the lessons learned, applying them to our lives and, in turn, passing them on to future generations. This ongoing dialogue enriches our understanding of the world and our place within it, fostering a sense of shared heritage and collective growth.

Final Thoughts

In exploring the rich tapestry of Norse myths, we gain more than knowledge of ancient tales; we acquire a deeper understanding of ourselves and the world around us. The enduring themes of courage, honor, fate, and resilience offer guidance and inspiration as we navigate our own paths. Let the echoes of these epic stories resonate within you, reminding you of the strength and potential that lie within.

May the legends of the gods and heroes inspire you to face your own challenges with the same valor and wisdom, forging a life of purpose and fulfillment. As we conclude this exploration, remember that old sagas are not merely tales to be told but lessons to be lived. Embrace the spirit of the Vikings—bold, wise, and unyielding—and let their legacy illuminate your journey through the ever-unfolding story of life.

By integrating the wisdom of Norse mythology into our modern lives, we honor the timeless connection between humanity's past and present. These myths encourage us to reflect on our values, our choices, and our impact on the world. They remind us that while times change, the fundamental questions of existence remain. In seeking answers, the ancient stories still hold profound truths, guiding us toward a deeper understanding of ourselves and the universe we inhabit.

Keeping the Legends Alive

Now that you've explored the fascinating world of Viking myths and legends in *Norse Mythology, Legends, and Legacy*, it's time to pass on your new knowledge to others who love these timeless stories.

By leaving your honest review of this book on Amazon, you'll help other readers discover the captivating tales of Odin, Thor, and Loki, and show them where they can uncover the same exciting journey into Norse mythology.

Thank you for keeping these ancient legends alive. When we share what we've learned, we help bring these powerful myths into the hands of more readers—and you're helping me do just that.

Your feedback means the world to me, and it helps more readers find and enjoy this journey through Viking myths.

How to Leave Your Review

Scan this QR code

OR

https://www.amazon.com/review/create-review/?ie=UTF8&channel=glance-detail&asin=B0DGR9DNSX

- Share your thoughts with other readers. You can be brief or detailed—whatever you feel comfortable with!

Thank you for your support. We hope Norse Mythology, Legends, *and Legacy* have inspired you with the powerful stories of Viking lore!

Best regards,

Shari Claire

References

Byock, J. L. (1990). *The Saga of the Volsungs: The Norse Epic of Sigurd the Dragon Slayer*. University of California Press. https://www.ucpress.edu/book/9780520232853/the-saga-of-the-volsungs

Clover, C. J., & Lindow, J. (Eds.). (2005). *Old Norse-Icelandic Literature: A Critical Guide*. University of Toronto Press. https://utorontopress.com/9780802038234/old-norse-icelandic-literature/

Clunies Ross, M. (2005). *A History of Old Norse Poetry and Poetics*. D.S. Brewer. https://boydellandbrewer.com/9781843840344/a-history-of-old-norse-poetry-and-poetics/

Crossley-Holland, K. (1980). *The Norse Myths*. Pantheon Books. https://www.penguinrandomhouse.com/books/330939/the-norse-myths-by-kevin-crossley-holland/

Davidson, H. R. E. (1964). *Gods and Myths of Northern Europe*. Penguin Books. https://www.penguinrandomhouse.com/books/319339/gods-and-myths-of-northern-europe-by-hilda-r-ellis-davidson/

Faulkes, A. (Ed.). (1995). *Edda*. Everyman. https://www.everymanslibrary.co.uk/edda

Gaiman, N. (2017). *Norse Mythology*. W.W. Norton & Company. https://wwnorton.com/books/9780393609097

Grimm, J. (2014). *Teutonic Mythology* (4 Volumes). Dover Publications. (Original work published 1883-1888). https://store.doverpublications.com/0486460252.html

Larrington, C. (Trans.). (1996). *The Poetic Edda*. Oxford University Press. https://global.oup.com/academic/product/the-poetic-edda-9780199675340

Lindow, J. (2002). *Norse Mythology: A Guide to the Gods, Heroes, Rituals, and Beliefs*. Oxford University Press. https://global.oup.com/academic/product/norse-mythology-9780195153828

Mitchell, S. A. (2011). *Witchcraft and Magic in the Nordic Middle Ages*. University of Pennsylvania Press. https://www.upenn.edu/pennpress/book/14969.html

Orchard, A. (1997). *Dictionary of Norse Myth and Legend*. Cassell. https://www.bloomsbury.com/us/dictionary-of-norse-myth-and-legend-9781848327284/

Page, R. I. (1990). *Norse Myths*. British Museum Press. https://www.britishmuseumshoponline.org/norse-myths.html

Price, N. (2019). *The Viking Way: Magic and Mind in Late Iron Age Scandinavia* (2nd ed.). Oxbow Books. https://www.oxbowbooks.com/oxbow/the-viking-way.html

Quinn, J. (Ed.). (2016). *The Routledge Research Companion to the Medieval Icelandic Sagas*. Routledge. https://www.routledge.com/The-Routledge-Research-Companion-to-the-Medieval-Icelandic-Sagas/Quinn-Lethbridge-Schorn/p/book/9781472462560

Simek, R. (1993). *Dictionary of Northern Mythology*. D.S. Brewer. https://boydellandbrewer.com/9780859915137/dictionary-of-northern-mythology/

Snorri Sturluson. (2005). *The Prose Edda* (J. L. Byock, Trans.). Penguin Classics. https://www.penguinrandomhouse.com/books/287922/the-prose-edda-by-snorri-sturluson/

Ström, F. (1985). *Norse Religion in the Viking Age*. Vitterhets Historie och Antikvitets Akademien. https://www.bokborsen.se/view/Folke-Str%C3%B6m/Norse-Religion-In-The-Viking-Age/8479677

Tacitus, C. (1999). *Germania* (J. B. Rives, Trans.). Clarendon Press. https://global.oup.com/academic/product/tacitus-germania-9780199240005

Thorsson, E. (1987). *Runelore: The Magic, History, and Hidden Codes of the Runes*. Weiser Books. https://redwheelweiser.com/detail.html?id=9780877286677

Turville-Petre, E. O. G. (1964). *Myth and Religion of the North: The Religion of Ancient Scandinavia*. Holt, Rinehart, and Winston. https://www.amazon.com/Myth-Religion-North-Ancient-Scandinavia/dp/0837182882

Völk, M. (2010). *The Norse Myths: Gods of the Vikings*. Michael O'Mara Books. https://www.mombooks.com/book/the-norse-myths/

Wells, P. S. (2008). *Barbarians to Angels: The Dark Ages Reconsidered*. W.W. Norton & Company. https://wwnorton.com/books/9780393060751

Wanner, K. J. (2009). *Snorri Sturluson and the Edda: The Conversion of Cultural Capital in Medieval Scandinavia*. University of Toronto

Press. https://utorontopress.com/9780802099471/snorri-sturluson-and-the-edda/

YEARBUCK. (2024, January 4). *The Hobbit Pdf Download.* YEARBUCK. https://yearbuck.com/the-hobbit-pdf/

Zimmer, H. (2005). *Myths and Symbols in Indian Art and Civilization.* Princeton University Press. (Note: While focused on Indian mythology, Zimmer's comparative mythological analysis provides valuable insights). https://press.princeton.edu/books/paperback/9780691017785/myths-and-symbols-in-indian-art-and-civilization

Made in the USA
Monee, IL
06 December 2024

72753839R00125